Liturgy for the Whole Church

LITURGY
FOR THE
WHOLE CHURCH

RESOURCES FOR
MULTIGENERATIONAL WORSHIP

SUSAN K. BOCK

CHURCH PUBLISHING INCORPORATED
New York

For my mother,
Patricia,
who taught me the beauty of words and the wonders of faith.

Library of Congress Cataloging-in-Publication Data

Bock, Susan K.
Liturgy for the whole church : resources for multigenerational worship / Susan K. Bock.
    p.   cm.
ISBN 978-0-89869-602-8 (pbk.)
1. Worship programs. I. Title.
BV198.B57 2008
264—dc22

2008016788

Printed in the United States of America.

Cover design by Brenda Klinger
Interior design by Vicki K. Black

Church Publishing Incorporated
445 Fifth Avenue
New York, NY 10016
www.churchpublishing.org

5 4 3 2 1

CONTENTS

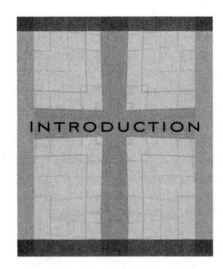

Church is for the Child

Not the four- or nine- or twelve-year-old child. Church is for that tender, brave, soulful part of us all that we bring from heaven and mostly bury on the way to adulthood. Because this "childlikeness" is divine and eternal, utterly open to beauty, awe, and love, Jesus says we adults must turn and go back for it if we would lay hold of heaven's treasures.

The Child Jesus is the archetype for that childlikeness which is the spiritual birthright of each of us. Each of us has, like Jesus, a miraculous beginning, heralded by angels and stars, a heavenly voice naming us "Beloved," and a special calling and place in the world. Each of us has, within, a Child that is imaginative, intuitive, and wise. A Child who is wide open to adventure, surprise, and joy, irrepressibly and seriously playful, but not childish and cute. A Child who is wildly generous and forgives quickly, "from the heart." A Child who is impatient with logic, but very much at home with symbol, fantasy, and myth. A Child who lives as though it were true that all things are possible, and who knows, as if by magic, the secrets of other worlds.

This Child has an uncannily accurate sensitivity to falsehood and evil, and is attracted to the beautiful and the good. In fact, as Sofia Cavalletti writes in *The Religious Potential of the Child,* God and the Child share a "correspondence in nature" because God is love, and "the Child asks for love more than his mother's milk." It follows, then, that worship that is welcoming and hospitable toward God will be welcoming and hospitable toward real children and the Child in each of us, and worship that welcomes the Child is wide open to the presence of God. And yet, through ponderous, wordy liturgy, heavily burdened with dry rationality and linear thought, making body and soul "sit still," the church does not welcome the Child in worship. Why? Because children remind us grown-ups (who are in charge of church) how vulnerable we are. Their very presence threatens to open us wide when we have spent lifetimes closing off, shutting down, going numb, getting safe, and becoming dull.

Childhood and childlikeness are two very different things. Jungian psychologist James Hillman believes that our earliest years are, too often, dangerous times of neglect and betrayal, terror and dread. As we grow, we repress and forget that early pain and our extreme vulnerability, distancing ourselves from them by projecting an idealized "childhood" onto young human beings. Childhood becomes "a realm of the psyche," says Hillman, and we become alienated from real children who are painful reminders of its perils. Small wonder that we don't want children in church with us!

And yet, church is *for* the Child, for the wide awake, fully alive, deeply true part of us all that is always hungry for more of God. Church has everything the Child most loves: song, silence, and shine; stillness, smells, and sway. Good liturgy is a feast for the senses and a playground for bodies. It enjoys and celebrates, as children do, embodied life, even as it stretches the heart, opens the mind, and makes the spirit soar. It invites us to lift our hands, smack our lips, clap, cheer, dance, weep, wait, wonder, and lose ourselves in the thoughts of our hearts. Sadly, we adults refuse the invitation, and are embarrassed by the children who gustily accept it, swooping them off to "children's church" where we "teach them how to act in 'real church.'"

But real church is for the Child. Real church allows small Christians to see, hear, lead, and follow all that is happening. It welcomes home the Child within by washing, binding, and healing her wounds. Telling our story, again and again, real church re-members us to each other and sits us down as one, in safety, belonging, and peace. Real church shapes us all in the discipleship of Jesus to which each of us, of any age, is called. Real church is where grown-ups may follow real children to our lost childlikeness, becoming most truly open to God's reach and touch. Real church is *unreal,* broken and weak, without the children.

And so, we must turn, again, toward the Child, and toward our own real children who will lead us in that turning. This return will ask enormous courage of us larger, taller Christians, but, as Anglican preacher Herbert O'Driscoll says, if it were easy, everyone would just do it, straightaway! Most do not, of course, and the church as church is too busy with grown-up things to attend to the shy, soulful, wide-awake life of the Child. But it is for its own good and growth, and the life of the world, that the church must do so—because only the Holy Child can lead us all home to God's heart.

Liturgy for the Whole Church is intended to help church leaders design liturgy for children and grown-ups who worship together. It is my hope that the resources herein will engage the imagination of all worshipers and lead them, together, to the "heart of the *gospel matter*" through story and prayer. These resources will help worship leaders in two ways to offer liturgy for everyone.

First, there are the theological foundations for such worship, which may be helpful in gathering the whole congregation around such a goal. Second, there are dramas, meditations, stories, simple sermons, prayers, and congregational readings to use as they are written or to adapt. Most of these are for adults and children together. Some are addressed to mostly children, others to mostly adults, for times when children or adults gather separately. Certainly such times apart from each other, for learning and celebrating, are good and appropriate, but the weekly Eucharistic gathering need not be one of them.

I offer these resources out of my enormous, hopeless love for the church and its liturgy. I hope you will sense in them my own passion for the full enfranchisement of children in the church, and my conviction that children will lead us all to deeper, braver faithfulness. Please use, adapt, and enjoy them! May they help lead God's people into the childlikeness that is the only path home to God's heart.

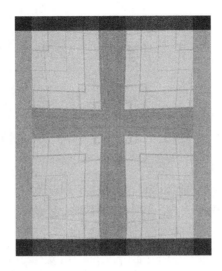

Children and Worship

How can we keep the children from disturbing us as we worship?" Wherever I have served as priest, this question has emerged. I have noticed that, as I get older, the noise of young children is harder to embrace or ignore. I feel annoyed when I have to mentally "screen" the sounds of cries, laughter, or talk. And things dropping. Again and again. And patent leather shoes running down the aisles. The sounds seem loudest at the most poignant words in the sermon, you think, but you're not sure because you can't hear and besides, you're mad! The only thing worse than all this racket in church is worship where children are absent.

Worship without children presents a quietude that seems out of place, and always scares and saddens me. It's as though the Pied Piper has come and gone, taking our treasure away from where it most naturally belongs. Church is for the Child, and children belong in church. So, instead of the question above, we might ask, *"How can adults and children worship together so that we all learn and love God as best we can?"* Put another way, how can all worshipers be respectfully invited and meaningfully engaged, addressed, and called by what goes on in our worship of God? The gift of God in word and sacrament is for each of us, and for all of us together.

The earliest Christians, who found the patterns for their worship in their Jewish roots, worshiped with children. Early church writings suggest that children may have had a particular place to sit at worship. Sofia Cavalletti writes that, since it is the whole Christian community that proclaims Christ, the child must have meaningful contact with the whole community.

Here are some practical suggestions for worship that will be genuinely inclusive of children.

GUIDELINES FOR PASTORS AND LITURGISTS

❊ Be clear, firm, and as non-anxious as you are able to be. Children belong in church. Stay with it, modeling your own joy and welcome, and others will eventually learn this truth.

❊ Reassure adults and children that all people are welcome in worship. If church school is occurring at the same time as worship, let it be an *option* for children and parents.

❊ Provide guidelines in the pew rack for worshiping with children. Some of these will be listed below.

❊ Remind the congregation, again and again, that at each child's baptism it has promised support to children in their life in Christ. This means, minimally:
- never glaring at noisy children or their parents;
- non-related adults inviting children to sit with them, and then guiding and supporting them through the service;
- ushers providing children with the same worship materials, as appropriate, given to adults, and never passing things, along the pew, over their heads.

❊ Consider a children's service leaflet that includes the whole liturgy and eliminates searching through several books.

❊ Always consider non-readers when planning worship. This means incorporating the use of repetitive phrases and choruses.

❊ Never make worship silly or childish, frenetic or loud, for the sake of the children. Children are more likely than grown-ups to enjoy, for example, contemplative silences and chanting.

❊ Never speak about the children as though they are not there (such as, "Remember when you were a child...").

❊ Recruit and train children for liturgical ministries.

❊ Teach children, in church school or in choir, special music or responses planned for a season. They can then help teach and lead the congregation in these changes.

Guidelines for Parents and Other Adults

These guidelines may be printed on card stock and placed in pews. They will be helpful to parents and other adults, who can be overwhelmed or frightened by the presence of children in church.

- Bring children to sit in the front, where they can see and hear liturgical actions and not just the backs of people's bodies.

- Engage young children by pointing things out. With all the bright colors, shiny things, movement, candlelight, smells and sounds and fabric, there is plenty to see, hear, and experience.

- Point to, or remind them of, responses that are about to be said or sung.

- Help distracted children out of the sanctuary so their needs can be attended to.

- Lead them back into worship when they're more ready to be engaged. Do this matter-of-factly, not punitively.

- Provide children with writing and drawing materials. They hear and see a great deal while using these things.

- And most important, *let children see you worshiping joyfully and eagerly.* Don't project your boredom onto them! If worship is boring to you, help your leaders to change it.

A Meditation on the Child in Church

This meditation is for adults, and may be useful for helping them learn the importance of welcoming children into worship. It can be done at an adult forum, vestry meeting, or other small group gathering. You should have a paschal candle available. Incense would also help the meditation, but is not necessary.

I invite you to fix your gaze on the paschal candle and to relax. Breathe deeply and settle into your body. Let the chair, the floor, the Earth, who is our mother, hold you up. She loves to cradle us.

Silence and breathing

Watching the flame, breathe in peace, making a big space inside you for your imagination to roam and wander. Breathe out tension, anxiety, the need to "get it right," and any other grown-up thought.

Silence and breathing

This fire is like the one burning in you, deep and hot, since the day you were baptized. On that day you were marked with Christ: sealed, branded, seared. That day you were adopted by God, celebrated in God's heart. The Easter flame has a life of its own, just as God's spirit has her own life, hidden away in yours.

See how it leaps and darts? This flame would never say, "Oh, I can't dance!" Just like this flame, the Spirit burns and sighs and stretches and dances in a secret place deep within you, yearning to be known through you, through the particular person that you are.

Watch the flame until you can see it inside you and then, when you are ready (there's no hurry), close your eyes. And with your eyes closed, continue to breathe in a gentle and steady rhythm.

Silence and breathing

Take some deeper breaths, and, as you exhale them, softly blow away some of the grown-up years. Imagine the flame, leading you back to a younger you. Gently breathe away a decade, . . . and then another, . . . and another.

Silence and breathing

Follow the flame back, back, to a very young you, one morning, in church. Maybe you can really remember such a day. The day of your baptism, perhaps. Maybe, as a very little one, you never were in such a place on such a day, but you can go there now as a child.

Just follow the flame, and tenderly breathe aside anything, anyone, any thought that stands in your way.

Silence and breathing

Can you see again how beautiful it was in there? The air smells sweet and strong. The space is dark, and cool, and hollow, but the sunlight is pushing its way inside, through deep, rich reds and blues, purples and greens. So many colors, shining gold and silver and creamy white!

Now your eyes are drawn, suddenly, forward and up, to something even more beautiful and bright than all that is around you. You've just got to go up there, to the tiny yellow flames, and silver, and the lovely cloth falling gracefully from a table, to see up close, to touch it.

Soon, someone touches your arm with love, and says, "Come on," and you are lifted high up into that person's arms, and your head is cradled on a soft shoulder, and together you are moving, ever so slowly. The huge white candle glows closer and closer, and brighter, and there is sweet, sweet song, and faces that are smiling so big, right at you!

You stretch out your cupped hands, and cool water is poured into them, and it splashes up onto the warm skin of your face and down onto your feet. Strong fingers are brushing your forehead with oil. A crusty piece of brown bread is placed into your hands and you eat it up, greedily and hungrily and happily. Dark ruby red wine washes it down your throat, where it lingers, stinging, and then warms you, deep inside.

And all of it—the bread, the wine, the water and oil, the sharp, burning smell—all of it washes over you like a wave of fierce love and belonging, and you know that you are wanted here. And safe. And that you will always come back for more. Again and again.

When you are ready, take a last look at the flame on top of the huge, white candle there in that holy place. Bring it into your heart, and follow it back, slowly, ever so slowly, quietly, to this room. Still breathing in a gentle, careful rhythm, invite the child you just were in your imagination to be with you as a companion and guide and healer.

When you are ready, open your eyes.

In response to your visit to that magical day in that lovely space, you may want to write, or draw, or sculpt, or create a poem. Here are some questions for reflection as you create your response.

❈ Before today, has the child in you ever been to such a place? What are your memories of it?

❈ How did you feel in that place, today, or long ago?

❈ Is there something you can do for the child in you to give him or her this sense of safety, belonging, and love?

❈ What does the flame in you look like? What does it feel like?

❈ Is there a child you could help to experience church like this?

PREACHING FOR THE CHILD

Preaching that is imaginative, that is rich with images and feelings, both everyday and fanciful, will be a proclamation that calls to the human spirit in children and grown-ups alike. That spirit, childlike and wise, listens for the truth it needs to hear. When "deep calls to deep," the age of the listener and the oratorical skill of the speaker matter barely at all. "Children's sermons," in fact, too often put young Christians on display, exploiting their attractiveness and reducing the gospel to cuteness and cliché. They are never necessary and rarely appropriate.

Anytime a speaker begins, "Once upon a time..." *everyone* sits up and takes notice. There are endless variations to this call to listen:

🎇 "It happened like this..."

🎇 "Imagine this!"

🎇 "Have you ever dreamed a dream...awakened in a cold sweat...wanted something so badly...waited forever?"

🎇 "It may not have happened just like this, but I know it's true, just the same."

When the preacher begins, "Today is the Sixth Sunday after Pentecost..." you can feel everyone slipping away into somnolence. Alfred North Whitehead believed that the greatest witness to the strength of the human spirit is the enduring of religious education! These words leap to my mind every time a preacher begins to drone, thereby sedating the ever-optimistic faithful, who return week by week listening for fire.

Reading Jesus' sermons—always simple, clear, and provocative—one can hardly imagine bored, sleepy listeners. It was quite the opposite. People couldn't get enough of hearing his words, strung together in poetic economy, stirring up hours of thoughtful wonder.

Here are some suggestions for preparing and preaching sermons which are more right-brained and thus more accessible to the whole community of worshipers.

🎇 Read the gospel early in the week and let it percolate. Ask children what they hear in it. Ask colleagues, neighbors, your mother, the un-churched, whomever!

🎇 Spend some quiet time imagining yourself inside the text. What was Jesus feeling as he said the words or lived the moments? Imagine how you would have felt or responded.

Remember the context of verses you're preaching about. How do the texts light each other up? In Mark 10, Jesus is assaulted by the deadly seriousness of the rich young man, who is urgently demanding the secrets to eternal life. Just before this, only moments, perhaps, Jesus has been with children, holding them, blessing them, enjoying their simplicity. He must have been shocked and bemused until the man slumped away, breaking Jesus' heart.

Begin the sermon by drawing listeners into the text. Set a big stage, rich with imagery that is familiar and irresistible: "Remember the hottest day of the world, and you were so thirsty your tongue felt like sandpaper, and you would give all you owned for the smallest drink of cold clear water? One day, Jesus was sitting alone by a well in Samaria." This creates trust in the listeners, giving them time to open the ears of their hearts.

When preparing, let the text preach itself to you. If the sermon doesn't happen in you or to you, it's probably not worth anyone's time.

Ask yourself the "bottom line" question: In this text, what is the Good News? Ask it again and again. Ask it one more time. The Good News isn't necessarily happy news, or sweet. It may be hard news, but it will ring true deep inside you and it will, at some level, liberate you.

Make it your aim to engage everyone, even if ever so briefly, at some level. Children and adults will tune in and out as they need to. You may trust both their concentrated listening and their blank stares to be signs that they are taking what they need from the preaching—unless it's a sea of blank stares for the whole sermon!

Don't be afraid to repeat phrases that are simple, strong, and true. Both children and adults may take these away as "mantras" to get them through the week.

Use your body and your face. When the text invites it, look up and shout. Whisper. Twirl. Sing. If you can, get away from the pulpit and your manuscript.

Avoid:
- Telling people what they already know.
- Complicated words or phrases that take the mind away to
     interpret them.
- Complete sentences. (They're not listener-friendly.)
- Overused Christian phraseology.
- Explanations of theology or doctrine. (These can be reserved
     for adult education.)

Find a few people whom you can trust for honest feedback including, always, children and teens. Keep learning and developing your own style. Seek genuineness and simplicity, not perfection.

✠ When you are finished, stop and sit down. Don't try to fill a time slot.

Sofia Cavalletti, in *The Religious Potential of the Child*, says that children are deeply and seriously religious, resenting triviality in matters of the spirit. Remember this as you preach for the child. Sermons to which children can listen, sermons they can hear, likely go to the "heart of the matter." What better thing can we offer to our sisters and brothers of every age?

Unless You Turn

A Skit for Grown-ups and Children

The small group of children are sitting on the floor and quietly playing. Four grown-ups are turned away from them, ignoring them.

Voice 1   Jesus said, "Unless you turn...

Voice 4   and become like a child,...

Voice 3   you will never see,...

Voice 2   you will never hear,...

All   all the truth you need to know!

Voice 1   The secrets of heaven!

Voice 4   The way to be human!

Voice 3   How to trust.

Voice 2   How to love.

Voice 1   How to see God.

Voice 4   How to live.

Voice 3   Abundantly!

All   Abundantly!

Self-satisfied enjoyment of a truth, grasped; then dawning puzzlement.

Voice 1   What does that mean?

Voices 2, 3, 4 I don't know; Beats me; (etc.).

Silent pondering.

Voice 1	I know! We could read some books about children!
Voices 2, 3	We could form a committee!
Voice 4	We could pray. And study the Scriptures!

Just then, they notice the children.

Voice 1	Or, we could just watch *them.*
Voice 2	And listen to them.
Voice 3	And do what they do.
Voices 1, 2, 4	*(horrified)* You mean *play*?
Voice 3	Yeah.
Voice 1	*(frightened)* And ask *questions*?
Voice 2	And ask for what we want?
Voice 4	And tell the truth?
Voice 1	And show our love?
Voice 2	Our sadness?
Voice 4	Our anger?
Voice 1	And depend on others?

They all look at the children, look at each other, ponder, look very scared.

Voice 3	Well, we could try it.
Voice 1	That's kind of scary.
Voice 2	Real scary!
Voice 4	Why do children do all that?
Voice 3	Maybe it's because they can.
Voice 2	And still remember how.

They ponder some more, then slowly "turn."

Voice 1	Maybe we could just be with them.
Voice 2	Be with them?
Voice 1	Yeah. You know, just be with them.
Voice 4	Maybe they could help us remember.
Voice 3	Maybe they would show us how...
Voice 1	to see...
Voice 2	and hear...
Voice 4	and wonder...
Voice 1	and ask...
Voice 3	and love...
Voice 1	and live.
Voice 2	Abundantly.
Voices 1, 2, 4	Abundantly. Wow.
Voice 3	Yeah. Okay.
Voice 4	Just be with them. Okay. Cool.

All sit and join the children on the floor and begin to play together.

Methods of Storytelling

■ Invite listeners to respond with a repetitious phrase when cued with a certain word or signal. (See a sample from "Awake My Soul" by Ernesto Medina on page 48.)

■ Use props that appeal to the senses, things that listeners can handle, smell, taste. For example, in telling the story of Holy Week, I've used a bowl with oiled water, rich purple fabric, a crown of thorns, pieces of rough rope, Veronika's veil, a sponge with vinegar, fragrant oils and linen.

■ Use the baptismal font and the paschal candle. You can tell the whole biblical story of God's saving love by standing at either or both of these and telling all the stories with water and fire. Splash the water a lot!

■ Tell a biblical story in the first person. To prepare the story, enter and live with it for a while:
How did you feel when Jesus talked to you at the well in Samaria, when no one else in town would come near you? How did you feel, lying on the road, your life slipping away, when the priest and Levite scurried by? How did you feel as the hated Samaritan started to dress your wounds?

■ Prepare a tableau vivant: this simple living picture is very moving, and easy and quick to prepare. (Several examples appear later in this book.)

■ Give each listener one line of the story, written on an index card. Have them arrange themselves in order (they'll have to talk to each other and cooperate!) and then have them read the story.

■ Give each listener one scene to imagine, then color and draw. Have listeners arrange themselves in order and tell the story, scene by scene.

■ Visualization works very well with children. Because they get so little chance to be still, they love to lie down and be talked through a meditative experience of the story. Leave a space at the end of the story for them to finish, either by telling, drawing, or writing it.
For example, have them join Jesus and the Samaritan woman at the well to share some cold, clear water. What happens next?

✷ Stop at several points in the story and have them tell parts of their own story, in one or two lines.

> For example, in the resurrection story of the disciples eating breakfast on the beach with Jesus, after the miraculous haul of fish, stop along the way. Say, "I remember a time I was so excited I did something foolish, like Peter throwing off his clothes!" Each listener then tells of such a time. Or, "I remember a time when someone who loved me made me a wonderful meal and it tasted like love." And then each one tells of a time like that.

✷ Have listeners write letters to or from the persons in the story. Read them aloud.

✷ Have the group, or each listener, write a newspaper report on the story, or conduct a news interview with story characters.

ADVENT

We are waiting, O God,
for the day of peace.
Give us the will to bring that day
through our own simple
goodness and hope.
Fill us with patient desire,
that our work may be holy,
and our holiness bright,
through the Christ
for whose coming we long,
and the Spirit in whose
presence we live.
Amen.

How Long Does Night Take?

A Story for the First Sunday of Advent

Advent is the night of the Christian year. As a Jew begins the day at sunset, so Christians begin the church year in the darkening quiet of ever-deeper winter, hushing our frenzy, readying for Christ.

When my friend Justin was very young, and I was tucking him into bed, he asked me, "Susan, how long does night take?"

What an amazing question, and one I had forgotten to ask for a very long time! At the start of the night of our year, we might well ask it now: How long *does* night take?

If you're sick and in pain, one night takes about a hundred years.

If you're alone, and waiting for love, one night takes forever.

If you're a child, and night seems a waste of perfectly good playtime, the night stretches on to eternity.

If you're a reluctant Messiah, sweating blood in a garden while the whole city parties, the night is terrifyingly long.

Night is all about waiting, and waiting is about helplessness. Waiting for dawn or light or hope or love or relief, we are helpless to turn back the darkness or hurry the new day. All we can *do* is nothing. All we can do is wait. But that very helplessness makes every time of waiting, if we will let it be so, a time of waiting for God. Every wait can become holy, artful, and lovely, a waiting for God.

We have no choice: Advent makes us wait. But Advent asks us *how* we are waiting. With anger, resentment, sleepiness, boredom, and despair? Or with desire, because waiting is all about that, too? Desire. If we let ourselves feel our desire and bravely name it, then waiting can become the birthplace of hope, and faith, and, especially, love.

Advent is the church's night watch, our season of waiting. The helplessness and desire in waiting make every wait, in the end, a wait for God. The good news of Advent is that if we wait, while we wait, in the waiting, God comes. The waiting itself is the thing, the very place we can meet God anew.

I'm terrible at waiting! I hate to be put on hold on the phone, or held back by a slow driver, or made to wait in the grocery line. And our instant, hurry-up world doesn't teach me patience.

But waiting is "mysteriously necessary to all that is becoming,"* and especially to the becoming of souls. So every time of waiting is soul-work, and a wait for God.

I once heard of a ninety-five-year-old woman who fell in the snow on her way to church and couldn't get up. She could have become angry, frightened, and cold. She could have given up, fallen asleep. She could have died! Instead, she made snow angels. She filled up her waiting with energy and action, beauty and warmth, and it kept her alive.

Near his end, approaching Jerusalem, Jesus gives us a clue to such brave and holy, artful waiting. The people are full of Passover joy in the hope a messiah will come, but he, sensing danger, is waiting with dread. Trudging along he sees a fig tree, heavy with buds, and his eyes are drawn upward where he notices, suddenly, spring. Remembering the promise of spring, unstoppable after winter's death, he says: "When everything around you is dark with violence and fear, stand up, raise your heads; your redemption is near."

Stand up. Raise your heads. Look to heaven. Hold to spring when winter draws down your gaze and your heart. In this very darkness, especially here, God is near.

Every time of waiting is a wait for God: a wait for peace in the Middle East, the results of a test, the conception of a child, or that child's maturing; a wait for love, or an end to grief, or pain, or life itself, or the rapture of the Lord. If we will keep company with our waiting, keeping it warm and alive with desire and hope, keeping it awake, like a mother attentive to her baby's breath, feeding it with faith, if we will look up and not lose heart, then while we wait, in the waiting, because of the waiting, God will come.

How long does night take? When waiting is holy and artful, filled up with God, just long enough.

* Gertrude Mueller Nelson, *To Dance with God* (Mahwah, N.J.: Paulist Press, 1986), 62.

LIGHTING THE ADVENT WREATH

Priest The evening of the year is upon us.

People **We enter the darkness and wait for light's return.**

Priest We light one candle to remind us of God's light which has come to us all through the Christ.

People **We open our hearts to that light, and ask for help to shine with the brilliance of love.**

Priest We light a second candle to remind us of the light of justice in the prophets' words.

People **We open our hearts to the light of justice, and ask for help to create a just world.**

Priest We light a third candle to remind us of John, who calls us to wade in the waters of new life.

People **We open our hearts to our own lights, enkindled in baptism, and ask for help to carry that light into a dark world.**

Priest We light a fourth candle to remind us that visions and angels may still light our way.

People **We open our hearts to light from heaven, and ask for help bravely to believe in our dreams.**

A hymn may be sung while the candles are lit and the lights in the nave come up.

Priest All of our waiting is a waiting for God.

People **God of our hearts, we wait for you alone.**

COLLECTS FOR ADVENT

Collects with young children can be done one phrase at a time, with the people repeating each phrase like an echo.

Dear God, we love you.
We thank you for loving us.
Help us get ready for Jesus.
Help us say "Yes," like Mary.
We are wide awake!
We are watching and waiting!
We pray with the Spirit.
Amen.

Wake us up, Lord!
Shake off the sleepiness
that keeps us from loving you
and serving your people.
Find us ready and awake,
mindful and alert.
Open wide our ears and hearts and hands.
We pray through the Christ
who is always coming among us.
Amen.

An Affirmation of Faith for Advent

We believe in God,
who bends and kneels toward our world,
drenching it with love,
making it new with every breath.
    We believe!

We believe in Jesus,
God become human,
who brought every person
a spark of the divine.
    We believe!

We believe in the Spirit,
hovering God, present among us,
abiding, upholding,
awaking all things to her grace.
    We believe!

We believe we are called to do justice,
love kindness, and walk humbly
with God and each other,
ready for God's reign, awake and alert,
as we work to bring it near.
    We believe!

We believe we are called,
as Christmas comes close,
to lift up our hearts in hope and in love,
seeking God's advent
in each moment and person,
each challenge and heartache,
each blessing and joy.
    We believe!

This we promise to do.
Keep us faithful, Lord Jesus, and come soon.
    Come soon! Amen.

The Prayers of the People for Advent

God of the prophets, give your church courage to speak truth, and to tell of your love.
    God of the prophets, hear us and help us!

God of the angels, give your church voice to sing your presence into the world. Give the world a freedom song, and help us to speak peace throughout the earth.
    God of the angels, hear us and help us!

God of Mary and Elizabeth, give your church grace to be pregnant with hope and to bring forth new life for a barren world.
    God of our mothers, hear us and help us!

God of Zechariah and Joseph, give your church dreams and visions, and the courage to follow them.
    God of our fathers, hear us and help us!

God of the shepherds, give your church humility, and to all who sit in darkness, alone and afraid, a light from heaven proclaiming peace.
    God of the shepherds, hear us and help us!

God of the magi, give your church gifts, and the will to leave home to find you among the poor.
    God of the magi, hear us and help us!

God of the Holy Innocents, give your church power to stand against violence and to protect the powerless.
    God of the victim, hear us and help us!

God our Sovereign, you are always coming into the world. Come to us now, soon, and forever, and let us receive you as the Child of holiness and the Wind of change, through whom, this night, we pray.
    Amen.

A Confession for Advent

Deacon   Emmanuel, we want to believe you are with us dwelling in this and every moment,

People   **But we pine for the past and rush toward the future.**

Deacon   We want to be found wide awake, alert with love, as you appear in this and every moment,

People   **But we slumber through and laze away the miracle of ordinary days.**

Deacon   We want to wait for you alone, with desire and hope,

People   **But our trust fails, our longing grows cold, and our hope dims.**

Deacon   We want to make room in our hearts, a safe and warm place, for you to be born,

People   **But we close our hearts, and harden them to you and your people.**

Deacon   We confess our failures at love.

People   **We are sorry; we ask your forgiveness.**

A brief silence is observed, after which the priest announces God's forgiveness.

Isaiah 61

A Congregational Reading

The people repeat the first response over and over, not in unison, but with the words "tumbling" over each other, and all coming quiet when it feels natural.

Reader	The Spirit of the Lord is upon me
People	**The Spirit of the Lord is upon me**
People	**The Spirit of the Lord is upon me**
People	**The Spirit of the Lord is upon me**
Reader	Because God has anointed me.
People	**Because God has anointed me**
Reader	To bring good news to the oppressed:
People	**God has anointed me.**
Reader	To bind up the brokenhearted:
People	**God has anointed me.**
Reader	To proclaim liberty to the captives and release to the prisoners:
People	**God has anointed me.**
Reader	To proclaim the year of the Lord's favor:
People	**God has anointed me.**
Reader	To comfort all who mourn:
People	**God has anointed me.**

Reader	To give garlands where ashes have been:
People	**God has anointed me.**
Reader	To give the oil of gladness for mourning:
People	**God has anointed me.**
Reader	To give a mantle of praise for a faint spirit:
People	**And we will be called oaks of righteousness, the planting of the Lord.**
Reader	For we will build up the ruins and repair the ruined cities,
People	**And all who see us will know that we are a people whom the Lord has blessed.**
Reader	I will make an everlasting covenant with them, says the Lord.
People	**So we will rejoice in the Lord; with our whole being shall we exult in God;**
Reader	For, as a bridegroom decks himself with a garland, and a bride adorns herself with jewels,
People	**So we have been dressed in salvation, and covered with righteousness.**

THE VISITATION

A Dramatic Reading for Two Women

A reader begins by reading Luke 1:24–27. The actors are not aware of each other and speak to the audience. The most effective thing is for the actors to come in on top of each other's lines so that the lines tumble, and are sometimes concurrent. They can choreograph their movements so that they move across the "stage" and end up close, back to back, or facing each other. Our actors ended by reaching toward each other and just barely touching each other's hands. It is important for Mary to be very anguished in contrast to Elizabeth's elation.

Elizabeth	*(happily)* They say you should be careful what you pray for!
Mary	*(with obvious anguish)* They say you should be careful what you pray for.
Elizabeth	For years we have prayed for a child, Zechariah and me.
Mary	For years, I have prayed for the deliverance of Israel. But I didn't mean like this!
Elizabeth	I can't be having a baby!
Mary	I'm hardly more than a baby myself, but this much I know: a girl can't get pregnant without the help of a man.
Elizabeth	But here I am *(touching the roundness of her belly)*, as certainly pregnant as anyone could be!
Mary	But here I am, pregnant! What will people think?
Elizabeth	I know what they'll think. "Elizabeth?! We thought she was too old!"
Mary	And the terrible things they'll call me….

The two lines below could almost be synchronized.

Elizabeth	Long have they called me barren! But God has remembered me and lifted my shame. The angel said . . . was there really an angel?
Mary	The angel said . . . was there really an angel?
Elizabeth	Gabriel was his name, and he said this child will be filled with God's spirit, even in my womb. He certainly is lively in there, and he's filled me with such life. And hope! Hope for us all. His name will be John.
Mary	His name will be Jesus.
Elizabeth	He will be great, and will prepare the way for the Messiah!
Mary	He will be great, and save our people from their sins. But who will save me from the wrath of the rabbis?!
Elizabeth	*(in an uplifted, heaven-looking posture)* I've always said, Lord, there's nothing you can't do!
Mary	*(in a more prayerful, thoughtful posture)* I've always said, Lord, there's nothing you can't do. So please, help me now.
Elizabeth	I have to talk to someone!
Mary	What am I going to do? Who can I tell?
Elizabeth	He never was much of a talker, my Zechariah. But now he's speechless. Claims he can't talk—the angel made him mute. Likely story!
Mary	I must go and see my cousin. Only, please, Elizabeth, don't condemn me!
Elizabeth	Mary! I could talk to her. She's young and hasn't waited so long! She probably still believes in angels! Only, please, Mary, don't laugh. But I want to laugh!
Mary	*(just a bit more hopeful)* Yes, I can talk to her.
Elizabeth	And shout, and sing. I'd dance if I could!

These remaining lines need to really topple over each other.

Mary	Please, Elizabeth. . . .
Elizabeth	Please, Mary. . . .

Mary	I'm so afraid....
Elizabeth	Don't laugh....
Mary	Don't condemn me.
Elizabeth	And come soon!
Mary	Please.
Elizabeth	Please.

A Magnificat may be read or sung here.

MAGNIFICAT

MUSIC BY SUSAN K. BOCK

The Angel Gabriel Visits Zechariah

A Tableau Vivant

The beauties of a tableau vivant are that they are easy and quick to prepare, they can use actors of all ages, and the group of actors can come up with its own choreography, although some suggestions follow. In a tableau, worshipers close their eyes and the reading begins. While the reader is reading, the actors are creating a scene. They freeze, a bell is rung, and the worshipers open their eyes and view the scene, in silence, for about ten seconds. The bell is rung again, the worshipers close their eyes again, the reader continues, and the actors get into their next scene, and so on.

The more variety there is in terms of age, gender, posture, height, facial expression, arm positions, and placement of bodies, the more interesting and "real" the scene will be. Even a ladder works well for adding height dimension. Big facial expressions and creative use of hands add interest; you can't overdo it! Quiet music may be played during the tableau.

Ring the bell, have worshipers close their eyes. The reader begins while the actors arrange themselves in the scene.

SCENE ONE

In the days of King Herod, there was a priest named Zechariah. He and his wife, Elizabeth, were righteous before God, keeping all God's commandments. But they had no children because Elizabeth was barren, and they were both getting quite old. At the time of the incense offering, Zechariah was chosen to go into the sanctuary and make the offering, while all the people waited outside and prayed. Suddenly, an angel of the Lord appeared beside the altar, and Zechariah was terrified, and overwhelmed with fear!

> *Zechariah should be up at the altar, one hand on the ambry, and, as though "caught in the act," terrified and shocked. Gabriel should be beside the altar, looking amused, confident, etc. All the people should be gathered at various places, "talking" and praying.*

Actors freeze, the bell is rung, and worshipers view the scene. The bell is rung, worshipers close their eyes; the reader and actors proceed as before.

SCENE TWO

But the angel said, "Do not be afraid, Zechariah, for God has heard your prayers. Your wife Elizabeth will give birth to a son, and you shall name him John. So many people will be glad when he is born, because he will be great in the sight of the Lord. Even before he is born, he will be filled with the Holy Spirit, and when he is grown, he will help many of the Jewish people turn and find their way back to God. He will be like the prophet Elijah and will help the people get ready for the Messiah who is to come!" But Zechariah said, "How can this be, for we are both very old?"

Zechariah and Gabriel are in front of the altar, talking joyfully, "walking" down toward the people (remember, they're frozen). Zechariah is expressing great wonder. The people have moved to different places, still talking and praying.

Actors freeze, the bell is rung, and worshipers view the scene. The bell is rung, worshipers close their eyes; the reader and actors proceed as before.

SCENE THREE

The angel replied, "I am Gabriel. I stand in the presence of God, who sent me to tell you this good news. But, because you did not believe what I have said, you will be speechless, unable to talk, until these things take place." The people outside were waiting, wondering what was taking Zechariah so long. When he came out, he could not speak, and they knew he had seen a vision. He tried to tell them, with his hands.

Zechariah is downstage with the people, who are gathered about him in wonder and concern. He is trying to tell them what happened, perhaps pointing back at the altar. Gabriel should be off to the side, watching, but easily seen by the audience. He is slightly amused and smug.

Actors freeze, the bell is rung, and worshipers view the scene. The bell is rung, worshipers close their eyes; the reader and actors proceed as before.

SCENE FOUR

Then Elizabeth became pregnant and rejoiced that God had taken away her shame. When the child was born, all the people came to celebrate and to hear him be named "Zechariah," after his father. Elizabeth said, "No, he is to be named John." When the people argued, Zechariah took a writing tablet and wrote on it: *His name is John.* Immediately he was able to speak again, and he began to praise God. The people were amazed and afraid, and said: "What will this child be? Surely the hand of God is with him!"

Zechariah and Elizabeth should be holding their baby and adoring him, like parents do. Zechariah has one hand up in praise of God. The people are gathered around to see the baby, and some of them are obviously praising God. Some are wandering off, pointing back, as if gossiping.

Actors freeze, the bell is rung, and worshipers view the scene. The bell rings, and there is a brief silence for contemplation. The actors should quickly and quietly disappear. The reader says, "The Gospel of the Lord," the bell is rung, and the worshipers open their eyes to a cleared "stage."

The Girl Who Read Torah: An Advent Story of Mary

Imagine. Imagine her wanting, with all her heart, more than anything else, the coming of the day of God.

Imagine the waiting. Hundreds and hundreds of years of it had finally taken hold in her very own dreams and her own deepest sighs.

Imagine her thinking she could help bring it, and knowing that, if longing were all it took, she could have gotten the messiah here herself by now!

She knew that day would be different than what the rabbis expected, and wondered if it would sweep right past them and they, with their heads all bowed in study and prayer, wouldn't even notice!

Imagine her studying Torah by the oil of a lamp, late at night, all in secret. It isn't permitted a girl, you know. But she had read for herself and she knew that the messiah would come soon and restore Israel, for good this time, and her people would be free. Free! From slavery, and exile, and oppression. Really and truly free. Forever. She knew this. But she knew this, too: freedom is bigger than most people think. And you have to be free on the inside, or freedom on the outside counts for nothing. And you, yourself, can't be free when someone else is still bound.

So she was thinking how the messiah might appear more simply and quietly than how kings and saviors usually do. How he might bring freedom to Israel from the inside out, somehow, from the bottom up.

Imagine her stopping herself in the middle of such strange ideas and saying, right out loud, "This must be why they don't let girls study Torah!"

But it's all right there! How could they have missed it? You just have to know how to read...between the lines!

Imagine the songs she made up while hanging clothes out to dry. Freedom songs, about lifting up the poor from their hunger, and relieving the rich of the burden of their wealth. Songs about freeing the captives...and the captors, too! Songs about healing blindness, especially the kind that can't see how things are, how they should be. Songs for the day when women and men could study and work side by side, unafraid. Songs of love that she figured God himself had written on her heart. Songs of love for the whole, wide earth.

Imagine the day her life changed forever, like it does with a baby, from that very first wave of queasiness. Imagine how scared and mad and amazed she was, recalling her mother's wise counsel, all those times, "Be careful what you pray for!"

Imagine her fear for the child, for herself, for what Joseph might do, and the names they would call her, the wrath of the rabbis, the hatred of all, the shame she would bear. Imagine her coming to see how all those dreams, so lofty and grand, stolen from Scripture, full of promise and truth, came down to just this. Skin, blood, bones. And fierce, fierce love and hope.

Imagine her, small and poor and brave, agreeing to such an outrageous plan, whispering "Yes," in spite of all reason, so quietly even she wasn't sure she had said it, though all heaven sat up and took notice.

Hearing God Speak

A Sermon for the Fourth Sunday of Advent

Various voices are assigned, to speak from their places in the congregation. Among them are God, Joseph, and Mary, plus five more who ask the questions below.

Storyteller	How does God speak to us? How does someone so great speak to someone as unimportant as me? And *why*? Why would God, who created the whole, wondrous world, want to speak to me, or to you?
	God's people have always wondered about this. Well, ever since Eden, that beautiful garden where God walked with Adam and Eve in the cool of the day's dawning. They talked together there, just like we do. But Adam and Eve broke their relationship with God, and, ever since, people have felt that God was far away, and they have wondered....

These voices can come from around the congregation.

Voice 1	Where are you, God?
Voice 2	What do you want me to do?
Voice 3	What do you want *us* to do?
Voice 4	Can you hear me, God?
Voice 5	I want to hear you.
Storyteller	Once, long ago, but long after Adam and Eve in Eden, God spoke to a man named Moses. Moses was minding his own business, caring for sheep, when he noticed a bush, all lit up with flame, but not burning! So he rushed over to see it, and he heard these words:
God	Moses, don't come too close! Take off your shoes. This is a holy place!

Storyteller	From the midst of the burning bush came a voice, telling Moses what God wanted of him.
God	Moses, go down into Egypt, and tell Pharaoh, "Let my people go!"
Storyteller	Later, when the Jewish people had escaped their slavery through the Red Sea and were wandering around in a desert, God spoke to Moses from a mountain. There was smoke everywhere, and loud trumpet blasts, and then, like thunder, with lightning, came God's voice. The people were not allowed to come near the mountain, or even to touch the edge of it. God spoke to Moses in the thunder, and then Moses talked to the people for God.
	Once God spoke to a prophet named Ezekiel. Ezekiel had a vision that no one else could see. It was a very wild vision, with lightning, and strange, winged creatures, and a throne sat upon by someone of bronze. In the vision, God held out a scroll and told the prophet:
God	Ezekiel, eat this scroll!
Storyteller	And he did, and it was sweet as honey!
	Have you ever seen a bush all ablaze that wasn't burning? Have you ever heard God speak in the thunder? I haven't. If God must tell me what I am to do, and show me the way to go, in thunder, with trumpets, through wild visions, I wonder if I'll ever hear. How will I ever know what God wants me to do?
	Today, we hear the story of someone who heard God more simply and quietly. Joseph was a simple, quiet, unimportant man, who was engaged to be married to a simple, quiet, unimportant girl.
	Now, if you've ever awaited a marriage, you know how hard it is to go to sleep. But Joseph had a terrible problem, so sleep came harder than ever. Joseph had learned that Mary was pregnant, and, since he knew the baby wasn't his, he thought she had been with another man. That night, he tossed and turned and worried and cried.
Joseph	How could this happen to me?! To us! *What* shall I *do*? Whatever shall I do?
Storyteller	Finally Joseph decided.
Joseph	I can't marry her. I won't!
Storyteller	And at last, somehow, Joseph drifted into a fitful sleep. But then, in a dream, Joseph heard God speak. God said:

God	Joseph, don't be afraid to take Mary as your wife, for all this is the Holy Spirit's doing.
Storyteller	When Joseph awoke, he never asked, "How could it be that a God who speaks through burning bushes and burning coals and thunder claps and trumpet blasts and wild visions would speak to me in the dreams of my sleep?" Because Joseph listened to his dreams, and believed them. And because he believed that such a great, loud God could come to him, little old Joseph, in the quiet of his sleep, speaking softly to his heart, he was able to say,
Joseph	Yes, God! I'll do what you ask. Yes.
Storyteller	And it so happened that Mary also believed God when God spoke to her through an angel, Gabriel. So, even though she was afraid, she was able to say,
Mary	Yes, God, I will help you. Yes.
Storyteller	God wants to speak to us. To tell us how much we are loved. To ask our help in loving the world. To show us the way to live, and how to be happy. The God who made the world, and who speaks from mountains, in thunder, from burning bushes...
God	Moses!
Storyteller	out of lightning, in wild visions...
God	Ezekiel!
Storyteller	that same great God loves us and speaks to us, to you and to me. Quietly. In a dream...
God	Joseph!
Storyteller	or to our hearts...
God	Mary!
Storyteller	or through a strong thought or feeling, or in the true, clear voice of someone who loves us. Quietly, so we can hear, and know, and not be afraid.
God	Don't be afraid!
Storyteller	Listen, always listen. Listen around you and especially within you and you will hear God speak, even to you.

FOUR CANDLES ARE LIGHTED

A Meditation for the Fourth Week of Advent

This meditation borrows heavily from Jerome Berryman's Godly Play *story of Advent, with the notions of a journey and its guides, and the statements of wonder.*

In Advent, we are all on a journey to Bethlehem. And even though we make that journey every Advent of every year, it's as though we've never before been, because our loves are always new, and so are God's mercies, new every morning. So we need to be shown the way.

One candle is lighted on the Advent wreath with the prophets, another with Mary and Joseph, and so on.

I
THE PROPHETS

The prophets, whose hearts burn with the vision of God's future, show us the way to Bethlehem. What is a prophet? Someone who sits at a Ouija board or in front of a cup of tea leaves and divines the future? No. That would be easy compared to what God asked of our prophets, Isaiah, Jeremiah, Baruch, Amos. . . .

Prophets are ordinary people who speak up for God. I wonder if there are any prophets in this room. The prophets of old were reluctant. They didn't want to say God's words because they were hard words, and the people were lousy at listening. But God touched their lips, or purified them with hot coals, or, in Ezekiel's case, gave the words on a scroll to eat, and they tasted sweet as honey.

Prophets believe in God's future, and can describe it with such beauty and hope that we can see and believe it, too. One day, the desert will blossom with flowers and flow with waters; one day, the lion will lie down with the lamb; one day, God will be near enough to us to wipe away our tears with God's own hand.

Even though there is darkness all around them, the hope of the prophets always lights their way. Ordinary, reluctant, full of light and hope. . . . I wonder if there are any prophets in this room.

II
MARY AND JOSEPH

Mary and Joseph, whose hearts are burning with a secret, show us the way to Bethlehem. What was it like to be heavy with a baby, sitting atop that donkey, so, so young, with a middle-aged, bewildered husband alongside, all plodding along to Bethlehem?

"What on earth am I doing here?" she thought. "Why am I going there, in the dark of night? I want to go home. I want my mother. I want my childhood, stolen from me, so rudely, by an angel who seemed too happy with the terrible news."

"What on earth am I doing here?" he wondered. "I want my child bride back. Innocent, like she was before all the wisdom of the ages settled onto her brow."

Mary and Joseph had longed so much for the Lord's messiah to come, for the ancient promises to be fulfilled. This was not what they'd had in mind.

I wonder, what is it like to hold in one's heart such longing for God that it brings God down in all the wonderful, terrible fullness of the divine presence.

I wonder, what is it like to be cast off from your people, shunned for the very thing God has given you, called you to, asked of you? To have a precious, impossible secret burning in your heart, pushing you on, step by dreadful step, so alone, into God's will and plan?

III
THE SHEPHERDS

The shepherds, whose hearts are bursting with newness, show us the way to Bethlehem. Their lives were full of sameness, those young peasants. Every night of every month of every year, they sat on a hill in the dark, singing the same songs, telling the same stories. The only change was in the canopy of stars overhead, which looked like a great hand turned it, ever so slowly, night by night.

Last summer, Cassiopeia was over there.... Now it's here.

It was comfortable and sure, their routine, but would anything ever change? Far from the centers of religious life, away on the grassy hills in the countryside, did God know where they were? Did God even care?

Comfortable and certain, bored and lonely, they longed for something, *anything*, to happen. They never imagined it would be so bright and loud! That it would change them, forever. That an angel choir would choose to appear to them, on the dark hills and not in the Temple, high and lifted up, where priests and scribes awaited such glorious visions.

I wonder, what is it like to herd all your loud and stubborn sheep to a tiny village and overwhelm a new mother with your wild, unlikely story? To hold that squirming, squalling, warm baby in your rough, brown hands, and feel him rooting against your dirty, ragged clothing? And to know, but not know, to feel that God has remembered you, and come to you? You, of all people, and turned your quiet world upside down with golden "glorias."

IV
THE MAGI

And the magi, whose hearts are burning with longing, will show us the way to Bethlehem. Their whole lives were taken up with desire. The desire to see. To know. The desire for truth. I wonder, what is it like to be so hungry for truth that you keep your eyes glued to the sky while falsehood ever-swirls at your feet? To be so hungry for purpose and meaning, for the Ultimate Truth, for God, that you'd pack all your belongings onto a camel and head off into the west, without a clue where you're going or what you'll find, knowing it will be true, whatever and wherever it is, and it will be your heart's desire?

But what if their longing *is* met, their desire filled? What then? You can't go back. You can't go home. Once you've seen what you've seen and know what you know.

Priests, they were, at home among the Persian people. Folks looked to them for the answers that they found in the skies. But they knew their wisdom had long since run out and that the final question, with its ultimate answer, the one that fills up the heart, can only be found on a journey.

I wonder, what is it like to be on a journey, committed to it? To be heading who-knows-where for who-knows-what, and suspecting it is everything?

I wonder, are there any magi in this room?

> *There follows a period of contemplation, accompanied perhaps by the quiet music of an Advent hymn. The session closes with this prayer.*

You are the God who is always coming to us.
Help us open our hearts to all you want to give us,
and tell us, and ask of us.
Help us to be willing to live with desire,
and newness, and wonder, and truth,
and to give ourselves up to the journey.
Come, Lord Jesus.
Come soon, come now,
come tomorrow, and forever.
Come, Lord Jesus.
Amen.

CHRISTMAS

Gift-giving God,
of angels and stars,
magi and shepherds,
promise and hope,
journeys and longing;

God who calls and sends,
blesses and guards,
hides and reveals,
asks and waits,
ancient love,
that is always new;

God of Christmas,
God of our hearts;
may we bear the Christ
to all who need him,
and allow his birth
in us again.
Amen.

The Prayers of the People for Christmas

Wondrous God, whose love was made flesh on this holy night, hear us, as we pray, and take to your heart all of our longings and thanks:
Hear us and help us, O God.

Wonderful Counselor, give wisdom to the leaders of the nations, that they might guide us to peace. Bring an end to war in the Middle East, Northern Ireland, Eastern Europe, and throughout Africa.
Wonderful Counselor, may your justice and righteousness be established on the earth.

Mighty God, make your church to be one, in spirit and truth, strong with courage and rich with grace. Help us to tell the sweet, good news of your love in all we say and do, and especially as we reach toward each other.
Mighty God, may your church be united in serving the world.

Everlasting Father, help all who suffer to remember your love. Bring relief, and strength to endure, to those who are lonely, dying, and in pain. Help, especially, those with AIDS and cancer. Stay near to those in prison.
Everlasting Father, may the day come soon when our tears are wiped away by your own hand.

Prince of Peace, help us to bring an end to all poverty and racism, which keep your children hungry and powerless. Grant that your peace would rule in our hearts and in our lives.
Prince of Peace, may you come soon to reign among us.

Child of David's throne, may all who live with you in glory help us, by their example and prayer, to find our way home. Give us, especially, the courage of Isaiah, of Mary, and of John. Grant us the wonder of the shepherds and magi. Fill us with the songs of the angels.
Son of David, make us one with all your saints who enjoy your presence day and night.

Wondrous God, thank you for the miracle and grace of Christmas. May we be true, all the year long, to its call to believe the impossible and to make our humble humanity the place of your dwelling. Hear us we pray, and take to your heart all of our longing and thanks; through Jesus the Christ, through the Spirit.
Amen.

Herod and the Magi

A Christmas Story

There are many ways and places to look for the truth.
> You can look in books, studying page after page after page.
> You can look in the Bible.
> You can ask around, and listen to what others think about truth.
> You can search the skies, and watch the stars align with the moon.
> You can listen to your dreams, and the still small voice within.

The important thing is to really want it more than anything. To want the truth, with all your heart, no matter what.

Because it isn't always easy. It can break your heart. It can take you far away from home. Or send you all the way back.

It isn't always easy. But the truth will give you something wonderful. Freedom. The truth will make you free, and freedom is worth everything.

Long ago and far away to the East, there were some seekers and lovers of truth. They watched the stars, night after night, following their star-journeys across the sky. They drew the pictures they saw in the stars. They asked the stars for answers to the questions in their hearts.

Imagine spending your whole life in such a star-gazing posture; it could give your spirit room to breathe and grow!

At the same time, in the West, was a man in love with power. The love of power is built on a house of fear, and fear leaves little room in our hearts for truth.

The seekers in the East were called magi, because they knew things, as if by magic. The man in the West was called Herod, because, well, that was his name. King Herod.

One day, the seekers in the East packed up their most prized and precious treasures, kissed their families goodbye, climbed atop some humpy, lumpy, smelly camels, and headed west. And all because a star, one star, one brilliant, lovely, constant star, like a diamond in the sky, had captured their hearts, and would not let them go. There was nothing to do but follow.

Meanwhile, in the West, King Herod followed his fears, doing everything he could to guard his little throne. And his heart began to shrink and shrivel, while his fear, and the darkness inside him, got as big as a kingdom.

When they reached Jerusalem, the magi went straight to the king, thinking that all great people hunger for truth and would be following the star and that a king would surely be leading the parade, happiest of all!

When Herod heard their words, "Where is the child, born King of the Jews?" he felt a stab of fear, like a knife, cold and deadly, right where his heart used to be, and he began to devise and plot and scheme, like there was no tomorrow. In truth, he couldn't imagine a tomorrow without *himself* in charge!

The magi followed the star to Bethlehem, and were overwhelmed with joy at the sight of the happy toddler, with whom they had a fine visit, while Mary, smiling politely, wondered just what does a new mom *do* with frankincense and myrrh.

And while truth lay quiet, for now, in their hearts, they followed their dreams back home, skirting Jerusalem and deadly Herod, who, upon hearing he'd been tricked, in his terror and rage, killed every boy baby born under that star. The heavens be damned, he thought, and truth, too. He *would* keep his little kingdom at any cost. And the world began to weep that day for those children, a weeping that can be heard to this very day.

But the child escaped Herod, like truth once had, slipping away in the night, unnoticed, to a lighter, more welcoming place, in the care of a man whose dreams wove round him, wrapping him in safety, like a blanket of love.

The people of God are called into a special relationship to truth. We are the magi who are asked to search for the truth and to follow. And when we find it, we are asked to leave behind all that we had or thought we knew.

We, like the magi, are called to adore the truth, and to give it the best that we have.

Truth is such a costly thing to seek—costly to find, costlier still to possess. But it's the only thing worthy of our love. And it's the only way to the holy child of Bethlehem, whose way is abundant life.

If you want the truth more than anything else, and seek it, and would go anywhere for it, it will come and find you, and give itself to you. But you have to learn to love it, and let go of the fears that crowd it out. You have to look for it in even the smallest, strangest, most secret and surprising places.

And when it appears, it will shine as bright as a star, and lead you to everything your heart has always wanted. And it will change you forever, and take you home, all the way home, by a whole new road.

A NATIVITY MEDITATION FOR CHILDREN

The storyteller begins in the dark, sitting with the children, with an unlit candle nearby. Also needed are: a large Bible; hay; lambs' wool; a long, long piece of gauzy fabric; a piece of soft fabric, about one square yard each; frankincense, gold, and myrrh, as possible.

The storyteller should practice with the long fabric, using it for a veil, a cape, and blanket, and, finally, a baby, to be swaddled in the square fabric and passed around.

Once, long ago, there lived a girl who loved God with all her heart. All her life she had listened to the stories of how God loved her, and her people. Stories of how God had saved the Jewish people from slavery in Egypt, who escaped right through the Red Sea waters that stood up to let them pass, in the dead of night. (Many very important things happen in the dead of night, as we shall see. I wonder if we shouldn't call it, instead, the "alive of night"!)

This girl was called Mary, and she had a secret. Girls were not allowed to study God's word, the Torah. But secretly, in the dead of night, Mary would light a candle and read and read of God's love.

Here the storyteller lights the candle, and leafs through the pages of a large Bible, wonderingly.

She read that one day God would send the Jewish people a Savior, a Messiah, who would help them in every way. Who would show them how to live so as to please God, and how to truly love each other, and how to come home to God's heart.

Mary heard the men arguing all the time about who it would be and when it would be and where it would be that the Messiah would come, one day, to God's people. She knew in her heart it would be soon. She hoped she would be ready. She wondered, sometimes, if the men, with all their arguing, might miss it!

One day, Mary was doing her daily chores, singing a song for Passover, which was just around the corner, when she suddenly realized the she was not alone. She was startled to find an angel behind her. She gasped, and then shrieked, and then froze, but the angel said,

"Hail, Mary, full of grace. The Lord is with thee." Which means, "Hello, Mary. You have a wide and full heart where there is plenty of room for God. Don't be afraid."

Which is a pretty odd thing to hear from a stranger who suddenly appears in your house right in the middle of your chores.

The angel's name was Gabriel, and he asked Mary if she would be the mother to the Savior they were all awaiting. She thought about it for a while, and even though she knew it would change everything forever, and even though she was very scared, still she said, "Yes. Yes, I will."

Mary and her boyfriend, Joseph, were married very soon, and Mary got huge with the baby inside her. As the time for the birth drew near, a law came down from the Romans that sent the two of them to a faraway city, to write their names into an official book for counting all the people.

As they were traveling to Nazareth, Mary rode the donkey for a while. Then she walked. Then she rode, then she walked, then she rode again, because women big with a baby inside can't quite get comfortable. By evening they arrived and began to look for a hotel, but every single one was filled with other folks who had come to town to write their names in the book. Finally, a very kind man said to them, "Why don't you rest for the night in the stable out back. There's plenty of fresh, sweet, soft hay, and lady, you look like you could sleep standing up!"

Here the storyteller should pass the hay and encourage the listeners to feel its texture and to smell it.

Mary and Joseph spread their clothes on the hay, snuggled up in each other's arms, and whispered about what this baby would look like, and feel like, and be like. They didn't have to wonder if the baby would be a boy or a girl, or what to name him, because Gabriel had already told them, and they believed in angels and the news they brought. The hay smelled so comfortable, and the animals snored deep and loud, and soon they, too, had drifted into a hard, long sleep. Or so they thought.

A few short hours later, Mary's eyes flew open, and she knew the baby would be here soon. Mary and Joseph were very, very frightened. They'd never read a book or seen a video or had a class about how to help a baby get born. Her mother was far away. But God was with them, and many hard hours later, their baby, Jesus, was born.

Mary took her finest, softest garment, and tore it up into tiny blankets for her son. And she swaddled him, like this, because babies love to be swaddled snuggly. It reminds them of being tucked away inside their mothers, close and safe.

Here, the storyteller will have been bundling up the fabric, and then swaddling it in the fabric square.

Some shepherds came to visit them all, because angels had come to the sky above them and told them to. All they had on hand for a present was some wool from their lambs.

Here the storyteller tucks lamb's wool around the baby's face and chest, and passes the rest around.

They didn't think it was such a great gift, but it was just what Mary needed to keep her baby warm, and to protect his skin. So often we think we have nothing special to give, nothing anyone could want. But sometimes that which comes right out of the middle of our life, something ordinary, something true of us, is the very best thing, and the one thing needed.

All through the rest of the night, and for many nights after, she looked at him. And told him all the things that were in her heart, and how much she loved him, and she even told him her fears for him, but also her longings and hopes.

Much, much later, some magi, following a star, came from the faraway east, and honored Jesus, like they would a king, for they knew from the stars that his birth was somehow important, and that he would be great. They brought him gifts, too. They brought frankincense and myrrh, very fragrant, rich, spicy gums, all of great value, though Mary wasn't quite sure what to do with them. The gold they brought may have helped the family escape down into Egypt when Herod was searching for Jesus to kill him.

Mary was young and poor, and she was only a girl. And in those days, to be young and poor and only a girl, a Jewish girl at that, was to be not much. Almost nothing, in the eyes of most. But to God, she was the just-right person to be Jesus' mother.

God came to her, and asked for her help.

She said, "Yes. Yes, God, I will help."

And God stayed near, and helped her be true to her "Yes."

And her "Yes" brought us the most amazing child, and all his love, and has forever changed all the world, as a simple, brave "Yes," from a simple, brave person, can always do.

A Child Has Been Born

A Congregational Reading from Isaiah 9

*This congregational reading was arranged by the Reverend Ernesto Medina. The people are invited and encouraged to respond to each sentence or phrase with the words or instructions in **bold print**.*

The people who walked in darkness	
have seen a great light;	*(polite applause)*
those who lived in a land of deep darkness—	**Oh no!**
on them has the light shined.	**Oh good!** *(loud applause)*
You have multiplied the nation,	**Yes!**
you have increased its joy;	**Yes!**
they rejoice before you as with joy at the harvest,	
as people exult when dividing plunder.	**Rejoice! Right on! Yeah!**
For the yoke of their burden,	**Oh!** *(as if in pain)*
and the bar across their shoulders,	**Oh!** *(as if in pain)*
the rod of their oppressor	**Oh!** *(as if in pain)*
you have broken as on the day of Midian.	**Oh good!** *(loud applause)*
For a child has been born for us,	**Yes!**
a son given to us;	**Yes!**
authority rests upon his shoulders;	**Relief!**
and he is named	
Wonderful Counselor,	**Wonderful Counselor**
Mighty God,	**Mighty God**
Everlasting Father,	**Everlasting Father**
Prince of Peace.	**Prince of Peace**
His authority shall grow continually,	**Higher and higher**
and there shall be endless peace.	**God's peace!**
He will establish and uphold it	**Yes!**
with justice and with righteousness	**Yes!**
from this time forth forevermore.	**Thank you, God!**
The zeal of the Lord of hosts will do this.	*(loud applause)*

THE CHRISTMAS EVE GOSPEL STORY

This story can be used in place of the gospel reading.

Long, long ago, before the time of your grandmothers' grandmothers' grandmothers, Augustus, the king of Rome, sent out a decree (which is a law that you don't dare ignore!). "Everyone in the whole wide world must go to their own hometown," he commanded, "and write their names in a great big book, so all the people may be counted."

He made the decree so that he could find more folks from whom to collect taxes. Imagine if our president said that everyone had to go to their own hometown to be counted. Northwest Airlines would never recover!

So Joseph packed up his little donkey, and traveled ever-so-gently and slowly with his very new and very pregnant wife, Mary, all the way down from Nazareth to Bethlehem. Along the way they talked about their baby, and what he would be like. They didn't have to wonder if the baby would be a boy or a girl, or what to name him, because the angel Gabriel had come to each of them with the news of his name: Jesus.

When they arrived in Bethlehem, all the hotel rooms were already full with others who had come to write their names in the great big book at the city hall. Finally, a very kind innkeeper looked at Mary, and wisely discerned that, even though she was about to topple over, she was tired enough to sleep standing up!

So he let them rest in the fresh sweet hay out behind his barn. Mary and Joseph spread their clothes over the hay, curled up in each others' arms, and, listening to the deep snores of the animals, drifted off to sleep. But not for long. Soon, Mary's eyes flew wide open, and she sat bolt upright, and shook her husband awake. "Joseph! Honey! It's time for the baby to come!"

Joseph jumped up in confusion, still half-asleep, and began to pace and wring his hands, looking for something to do. Only, there was nothing to do but wait. So he held her hand, and stroked her face, and whispered love and encouragement, and together they worked and waited, and waited and worked, until the baby came.

When he did, Mary took strips of cloth from one of her own simple robes, because that was all she had. No soft gowns or diapers. No layette. No rattles or pacifiers or Fisher Price intercom. No cradle or crib. In fact, she had to lay him in the animals' feeding trough, filled with hay, to keep him warm. As she and Joseph watched him sleep they thought how, in the blink of an eye, everything can change. And they really had no idea how true that was.

There were shepherds sitting on hillsides that night, out in the countryside, watching and waiting for the sheep to give birth to their lambs. Suddenly, brightly, an angel hovered above them. "Don't be afraid!" said the angel. "I bring good news of great joy for you and for all. This very night, the Savior you have been waiting for, the Messiah you have been longing for, has been born. Go to the city of David, and see for yourselves."

"But, we aren't dressed right!" they said. "What of our sheep? They won't let us in. We wouldn't fit, at the birth of the Christ."

"Oh, you'll fit," said the angel. "Indeed, you will feel quite at home. You will find the baby, in fact, in a stable, lying in a manger, wrapped up in the simplest of cloths." And then the whole sky filled with angels, turning night into day, even as this amazing new child would one day light up the world with his love. And they sang, with the sweetest voices and melodies anyone ever heard, "Glory to God! Glory to God in the highest heaven! And here on earth, let there be peace. Peace. Peace to all whom God favors."

Imagine the sound of that after sitting on a hill, lonely and bored, feeling forgotten, and waiting for something, anything, to happen! "Peace. Let there be peace. Be at peace."

When the angels had left, the shepherds said to each other, "Let us go now to Bethlehem, and see for ourselves what God has shown us through the angels." For when the Lord has shown you something like that, something so bright and clear and sweet, no matter how strange, all you can do is act like it's true.

Which they did, with haste (which means, really fast), and found the new parents all wrapped up in their baby, gazing upon him, like new parents do, as though he were a miracle—which, in fact, every newborn is: a miracle. The shepherds brought the only gift they had, wool from their lambs, but it turned out to be the just-right thing for Mary to keep her baby warm and his skin soft and dry.

Soon a crowd gathered, and everyone had to hold him, if just for a moment, for to hold a new baby is to be touched by grace and peace and the very love of God, from which that baby is so newly come down. And listening to the shepherds tell of the angels, all were amazed and wondered about it so loudly, the baby was startled and cried for his mother, who silently stored it all up in her heart, like little treasures in a secret chest, so that later, when she had some quiet time alone, she could take them out and ponder them.

And the shepherds returned to their fields, forever changed, and praising God for all they had seen and heard.

A Simple Sermon for Christmas Eve

A good pastor is never supposed to say, "Oh, I know just how you feel!"

But I think I *do* know how she felt. I know what it's like to give birth to your very first child. It's wonderful, and terrible, all at once! And I know what it's like to travel to a strange, new place, far from home. It's terrible, and wonderful, all at once! And I know what it's like to end a long journey, only to find no vacancies at any hotel. It's terrible and, well, it's just terrible! Especially if you have to sleep in your car.

About each of these things I know something. But to Mary, they were happening all at once, and that, I can't imagine. Where did she find the courage and strength, the love and the hope to keep going?

We have made Mary into a saint, sweet and compliant, lovely and lithe, with no hint of her frustration with all these hard things, or crankiness from lack of sleep or from her recent bulkiness and swelled feet. We always see her all lit up, draped in blue, a kind of superhuman or god. But she wasn't a god. When I saw a young friend in the theater playing Imogene Herdsman (from "The Best Christmas Pageant Ever") playing Mary, I remembered: she was just a girl. Seeing the tattered jeans and worn-out tennis shoes peeking out from the long blue sheets, and a young girl trying to hide her face behind her hair, I was struck by how human Mary really was. So young, so poor, and surely terrified.

Mary's mother was not there. There were no grandmothers, midwives, or girlfriends to show her how to diaper, or nurse, or swaddle. She was surrounded by men and sheep and cows. It's no wonder she was "silent, pondering it all in her heart." Who would she have talked to?

I know how tired Mary was after all that labor. How vulnerable. How she ached all over. How quickly she became a mother, and fell in love forever. How quickly Joseph became a father, all strong and protective.

So, so human is this drama. So laden with sweat, and tears, and kisses, and blood, and fatigue.

If I were God, I'd have done it differently. I'd have sent a Messiah to be born in a castle, surrounded by the best doctors, nannies, tutors, and bodyguards, coddled and safe, raised up to rule.

But this design is so common, so fragile, so…human. Just another poor, young girl and bewildered new dad, and a barn, and a feeding trough, and a squirming, squalling baby boy.

God comes to us in all that is most humble and ordinary, around us and within us. Not to some stronger, cleaner, loftier, lovelier, better persons or place. But to us. As we are. God comes to us in our own fatigue and grief, in those weak and shameful parts of us we can't seem to rule over. And in those humble folks who keep coming to us, or appearing on our streets, asking for food. And in the fears of those of us whose riches have bound up our hearts.

God hides in all that is most truly, embarrassingly, starkly, hopelessly human, that we might finally turn toward those things, love and honor those things, reach for and find God in those things. That is the mystery of Christmas: God hidden in folks like us. God waiting to be found in folks like us. God longing to love through, and be loved in, the most human of humans, just like us.

Amen.

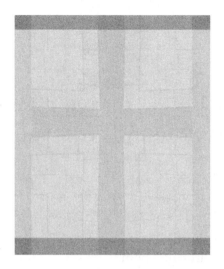

EPIPHANY

O God of stars and journeys,
you lead us day by day
to the joyful vision
of your light.

Move us by the power
of your word
that we too might
open our gifts for others
and so receive in our hearts
the child of Bethlehem.

So may you be praised
and adored, this season
of your Epiphany,
now and forever.
Amen.

An Affirmation of Faith for Epiphany

We believe in God
who said, "Let there be light,"
and there was!
With that light, God made the world
and all people in whom, and through whom,
the Light burns on, strong and true.
We believe!

We believe in Jesus,
the true Light,
who went down to darkness
to overcome death, and rose again,
to unveil our own brightness,
in the victory of whose love
a path shines home to God's heart
where all will live forever.
We believe!

We believe in the Spirit,
blazing with hope,
speaking the truth into every darkness,
warming our lives with God's gifts and call.
We believe!

We believe in the church,
where God's Light is praised,
and from where we are sent
to love and serve the world.
We believe!

We ask today that a gentle breath
blow from above
on the light that is in us,
the light that is among us,
and enflame us anew
with the courage of love.
Enflame us, O God! Amen.

The Prayers of the People for Epiphany

Shine in your church, O God; embolden us, in a dark world, to speak truthfully and to act with the courage of love.
This day and always,
Christ, be our Light.

Shine on your world, O God; heal the warring of nations and the wounding of the earth to give us peace at last.
This day and always,
Christ, be our Light.

Shine for your people, O God; make us one human family who clothe each other with mercy and feed each other with justice.
This day and always,
Christ, be our Light.

Shine in our hearts, O God; help us to reach to the heavens and deep in our souls to seek you, to find you, and to know you.
This day and always,
Christ, be our Light.

Shine in the saints and departed, O God; teach us to follow their lead to outrageous faith and eternal love.
This day and always,
Christ, be our Light.

Shine for the afflicted, O God; remind them of your deep compassion and how you tenderly bear all our sorrows.

Particular intercessions and petitions may be offered.

This day and always,
Christ, be our Light.

Shine, O God, as the Light that creates, the Light that calls, the Light that comes again with every dawn. Shine as the Light that scatters every shadow, and the Light in which we promise to walk, with your help.
Amen.

A Confession for Epiphany

Christ, morning star,
you ask us to shine into darkness
with your very own light,
but we cloud your brightness
with hatred and greed:
> **We are sorry, Lord Jesus.**
> **Forgive us.**

Christ, light of the world,
you call us to enlighten shadows
with lives brave and true,
but we hide our light
under falsehood and fear:
> **We are sorry, Lord Jesus.**
> **Forgive us.**

Christ, flame of God's love,
you send us with your fiery Spirit,
to gather and warm your people,
but we quench your fire
in cold, stony hearts.
> **We are sorry, Lord Jesus.**
> **Forgive us.**

For the sake of the world,
and our joy in you,
and all those you've given
into our care,
> **enflame our hearts**
> **and help us to shine.**
> **Amen.**

THE BAPTISM OF JESUS

This is a story about remembering. And how you might come to remember what you've really never forgotten.

It's a story to help us remember our own baptism because most of us think we can't. Most of us slept and dreamed our way through it in the arms of a grown-up who carried us to the cold waters that woke us only briefly and made us shriek with indignity! But if you touch your forehead now, and trace the cross that was made upon you that day, you might still feel it there, burning bright and true.

Remember the lightning scar on Harry Potter's forehead that marked him forever as "the boy who lived"? Well, see if your eyes can see, and your heart can feel, the glowing, the burning, of your own indelible cross.

This is what remembering can do. At Passover, the Jewish people are to remember the story of their great escape from Egypt. The story is to be told over and over, year to year, so carefully and richly, that each and every Jew knows that he or she was there that night, he, himself, and she, herself, passing from death to life.

At the Seder, the children ask, "Why is this night different from all other nights? Why do we eat bitter herbs dipped in salt water? Why do we eat *matzos* and *charoset*? Why do we eat reclining?" And the adults answer, "It is because of what was done for me, when God rescued me with a mighty hand, and brought me through the Red Sea waters, leading me out of slavery in Egypt, into freedom. It was for me."

To be a Jew is to remember how those great waters stood up to let you pass and came crashing down over your enemies, just in time. It is to taste and feel for yourself how the waters gushed out of the rock at Meribah, when Moses struck the rock and your dry tongue was stuck to the roof of your mouth and you were about to die of thirst (though you had plenty of breath for complaining and whining!). It is to feel the muddy waters of the Jordan River on your hot, tired body as you finally waded home into the land of promise, all green, fertile, and moist. It is to remember how you languished in exile, and sat down by the waters of Babylon and wept because you'd forgotten the Lord's songs.

A Jew could not tell her story without water—the watery chaos at creation where the Spirit hovered just before she began to make the world, and the watery death of the world in the great flood from which Noah was saved in the ark, and the waters of the river of God that Ezekiel could see, even from exile, looking toward home, bursting out of the temple doors. Even today, when a person wants to become a Jew, he or she must learn the stories and then be baptized, going under the sacred waters three times.

If you are born a Jew, already the waters of God's saving love run through your veins, but to become a Jew, you must go to the waters and bathe in them. It has always been so.

But there was a time, back in Jesus' days, when, to a man named John, it seemed the water in the veins was not enough, and that the Jewish people had lost their Jewishness through sin. He said, "Your blood, your birth, your history: none of that matters anymore because of your cold hearts. You need to come back to the water, and get born again, and get new, warm hearts."

And the people did. They were so hungry and thirsty for God, so sin-sick and lost, that they came in great crowds. We don't know why, but Jesus was with them. Maybe he just wanted to be with the people, near the people, on their side.

Just like all the others, he lay himself down in his cousin John's arms and let happen what would happen. And, breaking the waters as he came back up, God came to him like a dove, and he heard God's voice say: "You are my beloved child. You are my chosen one, my delight. You."

The truth of who he was flooded Jesus! In an instant he knew, unshakably, that he was loved by God with a fierce, forever love, and he knew what he had to do with that love. In a few brief, dripping seconds, everything changed for him forever.

Since that day, a Christian cannot tell her story without water—the waters of Jesus' baptism which were, in fact, the waters of the Red Sea, and are the water in our baptismal font even now.

In some wonderful, amazing, mysterious way, stories get all mixed up together in our hearts and minds. So that Jesus remembered the Red Sea and we can remember his day in the Jordan, and he and Noah and Moses can be with us at our baptism and today we can remember, and feel, and taste all those waters. When you come by the font, today, touch the water, and see what you can remember.

Can you feel creation's waters, and the water in Jacob's well, and the water Peter walked on when Jesus bade him, "Come"? Can you feel Jesus' arm around your waist leading you down into Jordan's waters, walking at your side, urging you on, going under with you, breaking death's hold over you, lifting you up to new life?

And you might have forgotten until just now, but see if you can remember and hear again how, on the day you were baptized, the heavens opened up to rejoice, and God reached down to gently touch your shoulder and said, "You are my beloved child. You are my chosen one, my delight. You."

In baptism, each of us became, like Jesus, the Chosen One of God, the Beloved of God, the Light of Christ, the Releaser of captives, the Healer of the blind, the Preacher of good news, the Servant Minister our weary world is waiting for.

When you have trouble believing it, or trusting it, close your eyes, touch your forehead, trace the cross, and remember. You are the beloved, the chosen, the delighted in. You. The waters have made it so.

Remember?

The Calling of Samuel

Needed are a narrator, God, Samuel, and Eli. Eli and Samuel are sleeping in different places. Samuel can be surrounded by stuffed animals that he's tossing around while he rolls and plays in his "bed," perhaps just in front of the altar.

Narrator	Now the boy Samuel was ministering to the Lord under Eli. The word of the Lord was rare in those days; visions were not at all common. One night, Eli, whose eyesight had grown so dim that he could no longer see, was lying down in his room. The lamp of God had not yet gone out, and Samuel was lying down in the Temple, where the ark of God was.
Eli	Thank God for the night—it's finally here, and I can rest my weary, aching bones. My bed, these days, is my greatest comfort, and sleep, ah, sweet sleep, silent and numb.... How did I ever get this old?!
Samuel	I hate the night! It takes sooooo long! Why do we even have to sleep, anyway? I wonder what amazing things will happen tomorrow. I wonder why I have to sleep in here. I wonder if I could open the ark and unroll the scrolls all by myself. I wonder how long nighttime really takes. I wonder why it gets so dark at night.
Narrator	Then the Lord called into the darkness:
God	Samuel! Samuel!
Narrator	And Samuel leaped from the bed *(Samuel should, of course, leap!)* and said:
Samuel	Here I am!
Narrator	And he ran to Eli *(our actor crept up on Eli, paused, and then shouted in his ear, waking him very rudely!)* and said:
Samuel	Here I am, Father, for I heard you call me!
Narrator	But Eli said:
Eli	I did *not* call you. Go back to bed, son.

Eli	Oi! Where does he get such energy? If I could bottle it, I'd be rich! Then I could retire, get an R.V., see the country, take up a hobby....
Samuel	I was sure I heard him call me. Oh, well.... I wonder how many stars there are up there, and I wonder where they fall when they fall. I wonder if I could swing from that lamp, like Tarzan! I wonder if Eli would get me a puppy. I love puppies! Or maybe a kitten, or a snake. I love snakes!
Narrator	Then the Lord called again, into the darkness:
God	Samuel! Samuel!
Narrator	So, Samuel leaped up again, and went to Eli and said:
Samuel	Here I am, Father, for I heard you call!
Narrator	But Eli said:
Eli	I didn't call you, my son. And I've told you a million times not to disturb my sleep unless it's urgent. Now go lie down.
Samuel	Sheesh! All he wants to do is sleep. I'm never getting old! And what's urgent, anyway? I think getting a hamster is urgent!
Eli	Lord, I'm too old for this. I remember being just like him... full of life, my ear pressed to your heart for a word, wide awake to the sight of you anywhere, everywhere. But it's been so long, Lord, and I'm so, so tired.
Narrator	Now, Samuel did not yet know the Lord, and the word of the Lord had not yet come to him. So, a third time, God called into the darkness:
God	Samuel! Samuel!
Narrator	And Samuel leaped from the bed and went again to Eli and said,
Samuel	Here I am, Father, for I heard you call me!

For these next comments, both Eli and Samuel address the people, as though they're thinking out loud.

Eli	This child has the most active imagination. Now he's hearing things, next he'll be seeing them, and by morning he'll have an invisible pal to whom I'll have to serve breakfast, and.... Wait! I remember nights like this... a voice in the night, calling my name. Could it be...? Oh, Lord, could it be you? Have you remembered your people, after all this time?

Samuel	I wonder if Eli would let me French braid his hair....
Eli	Could the prophet's voice again be heard in the land?
Samuel	I wonder why his skin is so wrinkled-y.
Eli	Could the seer again see God's dreams?
Samuel	I wonder how much longer till morning.
Eli	But Lord, *Samuel*? This wild-eyed, irrepressible child, a prophet? Well, I suppose that God will do what God will do.
Narrator	So Eli told the boy:
Eli	Go lie down, son. And if you hear again your name called out, say: "Speak, Lord, for your servant is listening."
Samuel	*(as if to memorize it)* "Speak, Lord, for your servant is listening."
Eli	Good! Now, go!
Samuel	*(as if practicing)* "Speak, Lord, for your servant is listening." "Speak, Lord, for your servant is listening." *(He returns to bed.)* "Speak, Lord, for *(yawn)* your servant *(yawn)* is...listening..." *(soft snoring begins)*.
Narrator	Well, this time, the Lord came and stood right there, and called as before:
God	Samuel! Samuel!
Narrator	And Samuel woke up in a flash, as only children can do, and said:
Samuel	Speak, Lord, for your servant is listening!

As Samuel and God take each other's hands or arms, they can begin to leave, perhaps down the aisle, miming an animated discussion.

Narrator	This was the how Samuel's life as a prophet in Israel began. Deep in the night, he heard his name, and he replied: "Speak, Lord, I'm listening." That's all he said. "Speak, Lord, I'm listening." And as Samuel grew up, the Lord was with him, and all of the words God told him to say were words that came to be true.

Whom Shall I Send?

SUSAN K. BOCK

Copyright © 2008 Susan K. Bock

composed in honor of the Reverend Sally Fox

A Meditation on God's Call

Names of listeners should be inserted as the meditation proceeds.

Each of us is called by God. To each of us does God call out, speaking our name: *N, N, N, N.* Clearly, persistently, into the broad daylight of utter innocence, wide-eyed wonder, and spring-loaded readiness, or into the darkness of nighttime, confusion, grief, despair, or bone-weary fatigue.

Each of us is called by God. To each of us does God call out, speaking our name...*N, N, N, N...* often a whisper, sometimes a shout.

And God calls all through a lifetime, even long after we've tried to retire God, or hide in the lonely, weary sleep of "I've had enough," "I've done enough...tried too hard, know too much...." Still God calls out our name...*N, N, N, N...* speaking heart to heart, though sometimes it takes another, softer heart, to awaken us to its sound.

And, while the *way-too-grown-up heart* has a thousand excuses and protests—
    Now wait a minute!
    I can't do that!
    You can't mean me.
    I haven't gone to seminary.
    I'm not trained, licensed, ordained, certified.
    I don't speak in public.
    I don't dance, sing, pray out loud, feel comfortable with adults, kids....

—the childlike heart, alert with wonder, impatient with the constraints of the night, leaps up, thrusts its arm heavenward, and says, over and over again, "Here I am! Here! Over here! You called?"

Always God's call disturbs our sleep: notice both Samuel and Eli spent much of the night awake! God's call always disturbs the sleepiness of habit and schedules and routines, the deadly somnolence of resentment or dearly cherished opinions. God's voice always gets us up on our feet, and pulls us out of the soft, warm beds of complacency and fear.

Often the call begins with the simplest exchange:
    "Charles...."
    "Here I am."
    "It's me, God."

"Oh?...*Oh*."
"Don't be afraid."

In the Bible, when God calls, especially through an angel, there's always the promise, "There's nothing to fear."

"*N, N, N, N,*...leave your fear. Walk past it, or around it, or through it, but leave it behind. I need you. And you, to be the fully human and entirely divine person I made you to be, you need to do and become all that I'm asking of you."

Each of us is called by God. To each of us does God call out, speaking our name.

And it may be that God calls daily. Or even all through every day and every night, into our vivid dreams, tugging at our hearts, touching our shoulder, blotting our tears, in a gaze across a table, into stark terror, through a closed or closing door, in a persistent idea, a Saturday workshop, a simple soft word, or a knock upside the head.

Each of us is invited into an intimacy with God where Lover and Beloved may speak and be heard, in a love kept fresh by constant call and response, call and response, call and response, until our whole life is Yes.

And perhaps it matters less what we're called to do, and how well we do it, and more that our hearts stay soft and supple to the sound of our name, spoken in unrelenting love, by the God who loves us enough to need us, and needs us enough to call and call, and call, and call again...*N, N, N, N.*

When each of us answers, the whole body of Jesus grows. We grow down and in, to deeper faith and braver love. We grow up and out, to touch every dark, sad corner of our world, sharing with it the love in which it is meant to luxuriate.

And it all begins with the sound of a name. Samuel...Samuel!

And the simple response: Here! Here I am! You called?

So listen. Close your eyes and listen now, if you like. Hear the sound of your name, spoken in love, from the heart of your God, whose days are filled with thoughts of you, and who calls to you, singing your name into the world like a song.

The Feast of the Presentation

A Tableau Vivant

The beauties of a tableau vivant are that they are easy and quick to prepare, they can use actors of all ages, and the group of actors can come up with its own choreography, although some suggestions follow. In a tableau, worshipers close their eyes and the reading begins. While the reader is reading, the actors are creating a scene. They freeze, a bell is rung, the worshipers open their eyes and view the scene, in silence, for about ten seconds. The bell is rung again, the worshipers close their eyes again, the reader continues, and the actors get into their next scene, and so on.

The more variety there is in terms of age, gender, posture, height, facial expression, arm positions, and placement of bodies, the more interesting and "real" will be the scene. Even a ladder works well for adding height dimension. Big facial expressions and creative use of hands add interest; you can't overdo it! Quiet music may be played during the tableau.

Ring the bell, have worshipers close their eyes. The reader begins while the actors arrange themselves in the scene.

SCENE ONE

When the time came for their purification according to the law of Moses, they brought him up to Jerusalem to present him to the Lord (as it is written in the law of the Lord, "Every firstborn male shall be designated as holy to the Lord"), and they offered a sacrifice according to what is stated in the law of the Lord, "a pair of turtledoves or two young pigeons."

Here, actors should set a scene in Jerusalem, outside the Temple. Mary and Joseph, tenderly holding a baby (just mimed!), should be on their way up to the altar. There could be merchants hawking their wares, kids playing with marbles, people gossiping. Go wild! Make it seem alive. Mary and Joseph are probably feeling a mixture of elation and intimidation. Anna, who shows up later ("who never left the Temple") should be in the back, praying.

Actors freeze, the bell is rung, and worshipers view the scene. The bell is rung, worshipers close their eyes; the reader and actors proceed as before.

SCENE TWO

Now there was a man in Jerusalem whose name was Simeon; this man was righteous and devout, looking forward to the consolation of Israel, and the Holy Spirit rested on him. It had been revealed to him by the Holy Spirit that he would not see death before he had seen the Lord's Messiah. Guided by the Spirit, Simeon came into the Temple; and when the parents brought in the child Jesus, to do for him what was customary under the law, Simeon took him in his arms and praised God, saying, "Master, now you are dismissing your servant in peace, according to your word; for my eyes have seen your salvation, which you have prepared in the presence of all peoples, a light for revelation to the Gentiles and for glory to your people Israel."

Here, Mary, Joseph, and the baby would be up nearer the altar, with Simeon, perhaps, behind it. Simeon and Mary could be reaching across the altar, each holding or touching the baby, and Simeon is ecstatic, with one hand up, praising God. Joseph could be bewildered and guarded. Have Anna creep out of the corner, and starting to see what's going on. Change the street scene below, with perhaps some people, having heard the commotion, peering into the Temple.

Actors freeze, the bell is rung, and worshipers view the scene. The bell is rung, worshipers close their eyes; the reader and actors proceed as before.

SCENE THREE

And the child's father and mother were amazed at what was being said about him. Then Simeon blessed them and said to his mother Mary, "This child is destined for the falling and the rising of many in Israel, and to be a sign that will be opposed so that the inner thoughts of many will be revealed—and a sword will pierce your own soul too."

Here, Mary could be crouching down and holding her baby protectively, with Joseph between her and Simeon. The scene is sad, darkening the joy of the day. Add your own interpretation. Again, change the crowd, perhaps by having them near and some reaching for the baby, foreshadowing the need many would have of Jesus.

Actors freeze, the bell is rung, and worshipers view the scene. The bell is rung, worshipers close their eyes; the reader and actors proceed as before.

SCENE FOUR

There was also a prophet, Anna the daughter of Phanuel, of the tribe of Asher. She was of a great age, having lived with her husband seven years after her marriage, then as a widow to the age of eighty-four. She never left the Temple but worshiped there with fasting and prayer night and day. At that moment she came, and began to praise God and to speak about the child to all who were looking for the redemption of Jerusalem. When they had finished everything required by the law of the Lord, they returned to Galilee, to their own town of Nazareth. The child grew and became strong, filled with wisdom; and the favor of God was upon him.

For this scene, Mary and Joseph could be in the aisle, heading back home, and Anna could be standing on the chancel steps, preaching to a small crowd of amazed and curious people. She could be pointing at the Holy Family, with Mary looking serious, engrossed in the baby, and Joseph looking back over his shoulder, warily.

The bell rings, and there is a brief silence for contemplation. The actors should quickly and quietly disappear. The reader says, "The Gospel of the Lord," the bell is rung, and the worshipers open their eyes to a cleared "stage."

The Transfiguration

A Skit

Needed are a Reader, Moses, Elijah, Jesus, Peter, and the Preacher/Priest. James and John are needed as well, but they won't speak.

This skit occurs within a tableau vivant. Normally, for a tableau, worshipers close their eyes and the reading begins. During the reading, the actors are creating a scene. They freeze, a bell is rung, worshipers open their eyes and view the scene for about ten seconds. The bell is rung again, the worshipers close their eyes again, the reader continues, and the actors get into their next scene, and so on.

This tableau is different in that there is only one scene and it is interrupted for dialogue between the priest and the different actors. Other actors remain "frozen" during those dialogues. They will have a long time to hold still so recruit folks who can do so!

Ring the bell, have worshipers close their eyes. The reader begins while the actors arrange themselves in the scene.

Reader   Six days later, Jesus took Peter, and James, and John up a high mountain, for some time apart by themselves. And Jesus was transfigured before them, his clothes becoming dazzling white. Elijah appeared, with Moses, and they were speaking with Jesus. (Mark 9:2–4)

Actors freeze in a depiction of this scene. The bell is rung, worshipers open their eyes and view the scene for about five seconds. Then the priest intrudes, sneakily, embarrassed.

Priest   Psst! Jesus!

Jesus looks startled, then annoyed, signals the priest to leave, and takes, again, his frozen position.

Priest   I just want to ask you a quick question!

Jesus sighs heavily, and comes to join the preacher.

Jesus   Who are you? And why are you wearing those strange clothes?

Priest   Oh, these are what priests wear. I'm a priest.

Jesus   Ah, yes. Never much liked priests. They're not much fun.

Priest   Hey, it's not an easy job! People expect me to make sense out of things like "the Transfiguration."

Jesus   The What?

Priest   The Transfiguration. You know, it's a big church feast and....

Jesus   Feast? Great! I love feasts! Lots of good wine. Where's the food?

Priest   Oh, it's not that kind of feast. It's a big church day, and they expect me to get all the theology right, and to explain the parallelism with Moses up on Mt. Sinai, and how the transfiguration is a foretaste of the parousia and a witness to the prophetic tradition of Elijah. You know what I mean....

Jesus   Huh?

Priest   Well, what does it mean? To you. What happened up there, and how did it feel to light up like that, and to see old, dead Moses, and Elijah?

Jesus   That day on the mountaintop was a real turning point for me. Since my baptism by John, I knew I was supposed to help lead our people to freedom. But how? And then the most amazing things began to happen. Like when I stretched a small boy's tiny lunch to feed thousands of people. And *(whispering, amazed)* there were leftovers! And then I healed a blind man, and a leper! What could this mean, I wondered. These were things the promised Messiah would do! Could that be me? A carpenter from Nazareth?

Priest   Yes! It was you!

Jesus   Well, some folks thought so, and they followed me around by the thousands. But others were angry, and tried to hurt me, and even to kill me. I was so frightened and confused. So I asked my closest friends, "Who do people think I am?" "Some say Elijah, back from the dead," they told me, "or some other prophet." "But what do you say?" I asked them. It came from Peter, clear as a bell. "You are the Christ."

Priest   The eyes of a friend who loves you, who sees you, can be like a mirror for your soul.

Jesus	I told Peter that if this was true, it was going to be dangerous and hard, maybe even deadly.
Priest	I would have hated to hear that. Everything we'd worked for could die with you.
Jesus	I needed time away, to think, and to pray. So we climbed a mountain, my friends and I, and up there, way up high, I could see forever! I could see all the way back to Egypt, from where God had led us out of slavery. And I could see way ahead to Jerusalem, with all its dangers. I saw it all. And I heard God say, "You are the one," and I shuddered. But then Moses and Elijah were cheering me on, and God flooded me with so much courage and love that I guess I actually shone!
Priest	So, should I tell these folks about your own struggle to find your way? And how doubt and confusion, and even fear, are part of the call? And how God always, finally, tells our hearts the things we need to hear? And should I remind them how time apart with God helps us find our answers, and how our friends, speaking the truth, can help, too?
Jesus	Would you do that for me?
Priest	Sure. But what about the hermeneutics and exegesis of the gospel pericope?
Jesus	Trust me on this one.

Jesus returns to his place in the scene and freezes.

Priest	Psst! Moses! Elijah! Peter! Could I talk to you for a minute? I'm sure you heard what Jesus and I were saying....

The three of them, embarrassed to have been caught eavesdropping, protest with a jumble of words: "We tried not to listen.... I wasn't listening.... Were you listening?" etc.

Elijah	I was up on a mountain once, trying to speak with God. And I had to put up with a tornado, an earthquake, and an inferno, before I heard God, finally, in a still, small voice, out of a great silence. *(He looks back at the mountain scene where Jesus is.)* This mountaintop experience was way cooler.
Moses	That's for sure! When I met God on a mountain, it was wonderful, and when I came down my face was shining. But then I saw all those people, carrying on, dancing around some golden calf! I was mad as heck, and I knew it was going to be a long, hard trip with those whiny, stiff-necked folks!

Elijah	You ain't kiddin'! I thought I must be the only Israelite who really loved God and still hoped the Messiah would come. And there were days I even wondered. That day up the mountain with Jesus, I knew the waiting was over, and I told him so.
Moses	Me, too! I told him, "You are the one we've awaited forever!" He seemed really glad to see us.
Elijah	Hey, we were glad to help!
Peter	That day on the mountain, I was bone-tired, confused, and scared. But when I saw Jesus all lit up, and him and Moses and Elijah talking and laughing, well, I was terrified, and thrilled, all at once. I wanted to stay up there forever. "Let's just live here," I said. "I'll make tents! It'll be easy, and fun, just us. We don't have to go back down. Do we? But then a cloud wrapped us all up, and when we could see again, there was only Jesus with us, and it all seemed like a dream. So we started down, but everything was changed.
Priest	What did you learn that day, Peter?
Peter	Well, in all my days with him, Jesus taught me that life is full of mountaintops, but valleys, too. And that God is always there, at any height or depth, and that we need them both, the highs and the lows. Jesus taught me to live one day at a time, and not to get stuck in sorrow or joy, but to keep on walking, with my eyes on him.
Priest	He was a pretty smart guy.
Peter	He was my very best friend. And my Lord.
Priest	Well, thanks, all of you. I'll share your thoughts with my friends. But I think I'll just let them think I came up with them myself!

The three return to the scene and freeze. The bell is rung, the people close their eyes, and the reading continues (Mark 9:5–9). The actors should quickly and quietly disappear.

Reader	The Word of the Lord.

The bell is rung and worshipers open their eyes to a cleared "stage."

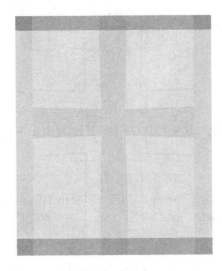

LENT

In this, the church's holy spring,
we ask you, O God, to renew us.

With a gentle breath,
blow from our lives
the dust of sin,
and make us your people again.

Lift us from guilt,
and shame, and regret,
to repair all we've broken,
and give us the gift of repentance.

With the lengthening days,
stretch our hearts, too,
to be ready for your risen life;
through Christ our Lord.
Amen.

The Prayers of the People for Lent

We pray for the church.
May she drink deeply from living springs, and travel the deserts in trust and hope.
God of mercy, make us new.

We pray for the world.
May we come to live as one family, and grow beyond the violence of war.
God of mercy, make us new.

We pray for this nation.
May we be healed of racism, and shine again like a lamp on a hill.
God of mercy, make us new.

We pray for our community.
May our children be safe, our leaders be wise, and our lives be peaceful and just.
God of mercy, make us new.

We pray for the afflicted.
May every sadness find you at its heart, and may there be grace when we suffer.
God of mercy, make us new.

We pray for the departed.
May they ever grow in faith and love, and may we always remember them by name.
God of mercy, make us new.

God of mercy, make us new. Change our hearts, mend our lives, and lead us to any who need us, for the sake of Jesus who came that all might have life, and have it abundantly.
Amen.

A Confession for Lent

Like the Prodigal, Jesus,
We have wasted your love.

Like Nicodemus,
We have crept about in darkness.

Like James and John,
We have slept through others' sorrow.

Like Peter,
We have denied and betrayed you.

Like Pilate,
We have washed our hands of blame.

And yet, as with the woman at the well,
You give us drink in the heat of the day.

As with the man born blind,
You open our eyes.

As with Simon,
You teach us mercy.

As with the disciples,
You wash our feet.

As with the criminal hanging near you,
You promise us paradise.

As with Peter,
You restore us in your love.

Give us, now, Jesus,
the gift of repentance, the grace of forgiveness,
and hearts made ready for Easter's joy.
Amen.

Jesus in the Wilderness

A Tableau Vivant

This tableau incorporates Psalm 91 and the hymn "Breathe on me, breath of God," for which the music is quietly played throughout and verses are printed in the bulletin.

The beauties of a tableau vivant are that they are easy and quick to prepare, they can use actors of all ages, and the group of actors can come up with its own choreography, although some suggestions follow. In a tableau, worshipers close their eyes and the reading begins. While the reader is reading, the actors are creating a scene. They freeze, a bell is rung, the worshipers open their eyes and view the scene, in silence, for about ten seconds. The bell is rung again, the worshipers close their eyes again, the reader continues, and the actors get into their next scene, and so on.

The more variety there is in terms of age, gender, posture, height, facial expression, arm positions, and placement of bodies, the more interesting and "real" will be the scene. Even a ladder works well for adding height dimension. Big facial expressions and creative use of hands add interest; you can't overdo it! Quiet music may be played during the tableau.

Ring the bell, have worshipers close their eyes. The reader begins while the actors arrange themselves in the scene.

Reader 1   When Jesus was baptized, he came up out of the river, dripping with water, bursting with Spirit, and knowing himself as "Beloved," "Chosen." The Holy Spirit led him away from the Jordan and out toward the desert.

The bell is rung, and worshipers view the scene. Jesus is strong, upright, exuberant, confident, etc. After a few seconds, the people sing verse one, while Jesus remains frozen in his pose.

> **Breathe on me, breath of God. Fill me with life anew,**
> **that I may love what thou dost love and do what thou wouldst do.**

The bell is rung, worshipers close their eyes; the reader and actors proceed as before.

Reader   He entered the desert to pray and to fast. He ate nothing at all for forty days and was famished, weary, and dry. He must have been terribly lonely. The cool, wet river seemed a distant dream. He remembered the psalms, and said them over and over.

The bell is rung, and worshipers view the scene. Now Jesus is in a whole other posture, defeated, weak, prayerfully imploring God for help.

Reader 2   Whoever dwells in the shelter of the Most High abides under God's shadow, and will say, "You, God, are my refuge, my stronghold; only you."

The bell is rung, worshipers close their eyes; the reader and actors proceed as before.

Reader 1   When Jesus' heart was very low and his body very weak, the devil came to him and said, "You don't really think you're God's son, do you? 'Beloved'? 'Chosen'? C'mon!... Well, then, prove it! Take this stone and turn it into bread."

The bell is rung, and worshipers view the scene. Jesus might be upright again, trying to resist the devil who is behind him, reaching to hold a stone in front of Jesus. They remain frozen while the readers continue.

Reader 1   But Jesus answered the devil with words from the Bible.

Reader 2   No one can live on just bread, and only God can fill us with the soul-food that lasts.

The bell is rung, worshipers close their eyes; the reader and actors proceed as before.

Reader 1   Then the devil led Jesus up to a high place and showed him all the kingdoms of the world. "I have power over all this," he said. "And I can give that power to you, if you'll bow down to me, and worship me." Jesus remembered the words of a psalm.

Reader 2   Whoever is bound to me in love will call upon my name, and that one I will answer, and rescue, and bring to honor. Not the honor of power, but the honor of my love.

The bell is rung, and worshipers view the scene. Jesus may be "sinking," that is, in a lower posture, perhaps of prayer, while the devil is standing upright, triumphant, powerful.

The people sing verse two of the hymn.

> **Breathe on me, breath of God, until my heart is pure,**
> **until with thee, I will one will, to do or to endure.**

The bell is rung, worshipers close their eyes; the reader and actors proceed as before.

Reader 1   Then the devil took Jesus to Jerusalem, up to the top of the Temple, and said, "If you are God's son, then throw yourself down from here, for it is written (the devil knew words of the psalms, too, you see): 'God will command his angels to protect you. On their hands they will bear you up, so that you will not even scrape your foot against a stone.'" But Jesus answered the devil with words from the very same psalm.

The bell is rung, and worshipers view the scene. This scene should be elevated where people can see, as Jesus is at his lowest, weakest, neediest, most vulnerable point so far and the devil would be even lower, trying to look into his face.

Reader 2   Nothing evil shall happen to you. No plague shall come close to you. Even when you are near poisonous snakes and young lions, you shall be safe.

The bell is rung, worshipers close their eyes; the reader and actors proceed as before.

Reader 1   Jesus finally shut the devil up with more words from the Bible: "You shouldn't test God. You should trust God's love to always help you." So the devil gave up and left him alone. Jesus was exhausted and weak, but peaceful, and angels and wild beasts came to care for him.

The bell is rung, and worshipers view the scene. Jesus may be reclining among a group of ministering angels and beasts.

The people sing a last verse of the hymn.

> **Breathe on me, breath of God, till I am wholly thine,**
> **and all this earthly part of me glows with thy fire divine.**

The bell is rung; the people close their eyes. The people could hum one more verse while the tableau disappears. When the bell is rung again, they open their eyes to a cleared "stage."

Reader 1   The Word of the Lord.

People   **Thanks be to God.**

NICODEMUS'S LONG, LONG NIGHT

One night, a night like any other, Nicodemus wrapped himself up in the arms of his wife, and settled down to a long, hard sleep. Or so he thought.

I remember such a night. Around midnight, I closed my eyes, and felt the very first pain of my very first childbirth. My eyes flew open. I looked at my sleeping husband, and I could tell it was going to be a very long, hard, scary night!

The night, you know, has a life all its own, with shadows and terrors and things reaching out from under the bed to grab your ankles. In the night your tooth, your ear, and the wounds of your heart hurt much worse than in daylight, and your fears loom much larger! And you, of course, are the only one in the world who's still awake, and morning threatens never to come.

Always before, Nicodemus had slept just fine. It was one of the things he counted on: early to bed, early to rise, and all that. And his days were well-ordered, too, with the hours of prayer, and the keeping of Torah, and the life of a righteous Jew.

But then Jesus had appeared and, with his astonishing words and ways, had called into question Nicodemus' whole life!

Jesus lived in such simple trust (well, he didn't own a thing!), and his gaze was drenched with love (and no fear at all!), and he spoke of a tender, compassionate God and, well, this changed everything! Now Nicodemus's mind was stirred up, and his heart kind of burned, and his belly roiled with questions. He felt like he was tumbling head-long over a cliff, like when you're falling in love, or having a baby, or wrestling with a dilemma, which he was, in fact, because Jesus had waked him from that slumbering sameness (which feels very safe but is really quite dangerous to the soul) and now he couldn't sleep and he was pretty darned mad!

And so, in the cover of night, Nicodemus slipped from his wife's embrace, crept from the house, and prowled the dark lanes of town till he found the place where Jesus was staying, and guess what. Jesus was up and awake too!

"Ah," he said, "Nicodemus, here you are, in the very dark of night. And such a lovely night it is, had you noticed?"

Well, no, he hadn't actually, because his sleep was disturbed, and tomorrow was planned and the next day, too, and the one after that, and how was he supposed to get through them, safe and stolid and sure, with no sleep at all?!

"Nicodemus, have you ever noticed how many babies get born in the night?" said Jesus. "I wonder why that is. And there are animals, and insects, and birds, and even flowers that only come out at night! Isn't that a wonder?"

So Nicodemus sighed, shook his head, sat down, and started to unwind. All through the night they talked, whispering of things all new, like wind and spirit and water and getting born and what really matters. And often the questions just hovered in the air between them, silent, gentle, and patient.

New birth and new life almost always happen in the darkness. The darkness of under the earth where spring is reborn, the darkness of deep in the womb where babies get their life, the deep darkness of a cave-like tomb where Jesus himself was raised to new life. Birth and rebirth usually happen in the night, in the long, dark hours between dusk and dawn, and certainly in the darkness of loss and grief, loneliness and fear, sickness and dying, growing up, growing old and just letting go.

Nicodemus was used to the daylight of control and order and predictability. But Jesus invited Nicodemus into the dark, moist folds of the womb of his heart, to wait there, awake in the dark, for a new birth that can only be given, and only from above. We don't know if he did get born again. He might have skulked and slinked home through back alleys, refusing the call, afraid of the dark, afraid to change, afraid to live.

But maybe, after this shadowy, secret encounter, he emerged, glistening and new, like a baby fresh from the womb, returning home by the new light of dawn, utterly changed forever. Maybe we'll follow him, searching for Jesus in our souls' dark nights, and waiting with him right there for all that God can do.

The Samaritan Woman at the Well

It might seem like the simple story of a thirsty man and thirstier woman, but it's really about the tumbling down of stony walls and love flowing free, like water. Listen.

Do you remember the hottest, stillest day of your life, a dog-day of summer when you could barely move or breathe and your tongue was sticking to the roof of your mouth?

On a day just like that, Jesus is resting at a well in Samaria, alone and exhausted, with a sad, scared feeling which he can't quite name circling his heart. So he leans over to listen deeply to the cool, wet echoes at the bottom of the well, and then scrabbles around for some stones to throw down.

Do you remember a summer afternoon and a moment of peace, when the thoughts of your heart could tumble and roam?

On an afternoon just like that, Jesus is pondering the well, how for hundreds of years it has sent up its cold, clear water to thousands of thirsty souls! If only he could get some now, he thinks, suddenly so thirsty, his mouth dry as sand, and not a rope or jar in sight! When he sees her, across the square, with these very things, he blesses the day and his ancestor Jacob, who gave them this well!

But wait—she's a woman, a Samaritan woman, and rabbis don't speak to women in public and Jews have nothing to do with Samaritans. And the well is where guys come to meet girls... what if she thinks he's hitting on her? And what is she doing here, now, when the other women come in the cool of evening... what's she hiding? And if he drinks from her jar, where and when will he be able to do all those elaborate washings...?

Do you remember a time when your mind wouldn't shut up and the harder you thought, the more mixed up you got?

In a moment just like that, Jesus notices her eyes, quite lovely, as deep as this well, which, he suddenly remembers, knows nothing of these rules and gives water to everyone: women and men, Samaritans and Jews, poor and rich, unclean or holy. It flows for everyone, anyone who is thirsty, and *just like that,* his mind opens up and a wall tumbles down in his heart, and he speaks. "Could you draw me some water? I'm dying of thirst. Could you give me a drink?" And she smiles! Well, it's not quite a smile, more like a smirk, but she lowers her jar and says, "You, a Jew, would drink from a Samaritan's jar?"

Do you remember a time your mind shouted "No!" but your heart whispered, "Why not?"

It was just that way for Jesus, as he begins the longest, deepest, richest, bravest talk he ever has with anyone in the whole gospel story. With a woman! And remember how, with Nicodemus, it was all that lofty, third-person stuff about the Son of Man? Well, here, with her, the walls are coming down, and pretty soon it's "I" talk....

"I give the water. I am the water. I am the well." It's the first time he's ever said such things out loud and she's listening, really listening, and his heart lifts a bit. But she's a woman, from Samaria, with five ex-husbands and a bad reputation, and she's shacking up now with some other guy, and she's about as lost as a soul could be! But they're both so thirsty, for water, sure, but for friendship, and connection, and God.

Do you remember a time your heart won out, and opened you wide, and gave you the gift of a love without strings?

It's just like that now for them both as the walls come tumbling down and they sit, in silence, knowing they are, from this moment, forever changed. He can't take back what he's said and now knows, and she can't go back to the life she's had. So they sit, and sip, quiet, wondering, refreshed, all new.

Then she says, "You know that old argument about the place of true worship? What do you say to that?"

And just like that, another wall tumbles down! "True worship is a matter of the heart," he says, "and you could wash your hands a million times, and crawl on your knees to the highest altar and God would be far less pleased than by a heart that finally, tremblingly, lays itself down in love."

Do you remember saying something so wise and amazing, you had to look around for who really spoke it?

Just then she does just that! "I know when the messiah comes he will explode all our sad, small notions of God!" And he says, "I am he."

As the words hover between them, clear and true, and the earth shifts under their feet, the disciples come crashing back, loud and rude and off she runs, leaving her jar at the well. And this nameless woman, once hiding and ashamed, is so changed that all the townsfolk listen as she tells about Jesus, and follow her back to see for themselves.

And he's so changed, so utterly sure, now, that God's love is too large to leave anyone out, even a woman, even a Samaritan woman, even a promiscuous Samaritan woman, that he stays to preach that love for two whole days in a place he'd once thought so foreign and strange.

Many townsfolk come to believe in this love, brought to them by a Jewish rabbi, of all people—will wonders never cease?

Have you ever asked yourself that question: Will wonders never cease?

He asks it this day of himself, and he has to say that, no, they won't. The wonders of God's love, he now knows, are as strong and unceasing as an ancient, everflowing spring, and streams flowing free, and raging rivers that drown our shame and fear while carving away the stony walls that keep us apart. And they are for everyone, those wonders, absolutely everyone.

Have you ever thought they might be for you?

A Story of the Waters

I invite you to close your eyes, because some things can only be seen with the eyes closed. Now, listen to the water. Just listen.

Water is poured, slowly and loudly, into the font. Throughout the rest of the story, create sound with the water as you are led to do so.

And go, now, to the beginning of time when there was nothing. Nothing. Nothing but deep, cold water, with a blanket of darkness stretching across it. The Spirit of God spent all her days hovering over that water, searching for something to love, someplace to plant her feet, and to be at rest.

Then came the day when God began to create the world. God spoke, and suddenly there was water above, held up in place by a great vault, and water below separated by dry land. If you listen hard, you will hear that water crashing upon the virgin beaches, and rolling softly away, in a gentle rhythm, crashing, rolling, again and again. The waters filled up with living things, and the earth and skies, too. And God made a people to love. And it was all beautiful, and noisy, and good.

Pause for silence and breathing.

Then one day, the rain came, soft and quiet at first, but then the windows of heaven were opened and the waters poured over the earth in a Great Flood. It rained and rained, three days, seven days, twelve, twenty, on and on, thirty days, forty days. Then God sent a strong wind to blow back the rain, and hung a rainbow on the mist that was left in the air. You might be able to feel the water in the soggy ground under your feet as you emerge with Noah from the ark. And you can't help but notice the rainbow!

Pause for silence and breathing.

Now you are walking right through the Red Sea, whose waters are standing high to both sides, pressed back by God's own two hands, and the ground under your feet isn't even damp, and just as you step safely to shore, you can hear the thunderous crash of the sea, back into its place, covering your enemies. And you can't help but hear Miriam and our mothers, singing and dancing, wild with joy.

Pause for silence and breathing.

And now you are standing by Moses as he strikes the rock and water gushes out of it; and you are so dry and thirsty, you can't help but try to catch it in your hands and splash it all over and around you.

Pause for silence and breathing.

Now you are wading into the Jordan River with all your belongings heavy on your back. The water is so cool on your hot, tired dusty feet. And stepping up on the far bank, drenched and dripping with that brown water, you can't help but know you are home. Finally, home.

Pause for silence and breathing.

And now you are sitting at Jacob's well in Samaria, at high noon, with Jesus, and he is telling you all that is on his mind, while you both drink the well's cold, clear, delicious water. You can't help but taste it.

Pause for silence and breathing.

Now you're with Peter, fishing in the water. Walking on it, now, reaching for Jesus, thinking this must be a dream. And now you're with Philip and the Ethiopian eunuch, up to your waist in a tiny desert pond, pouring the water over the eunuch's head and claiming him for Christ. And you can't help but say, "Amen, amen."

Pause for silence and breathing.

Before you open your eyes, make a promise in your heart to gaze into this bowl of water, and look for all the water I've just reminded you of. It's all in here.

Pause for silence and breathing.

And now, when you are ready, open your eyes.

In this water is the story of our life with God:
>From this water, we are lifted to dry ground, with Noah.
>Through it, we are rescued, like the Israelites.
>In it, we are carried home, over Jordan, into the church.
>In and through this water, we are drowned and saved, washed and sustained.

In this water, the story of God's saving grace becomes our story, too. From exile in Babylon, Ezekiel looked toward Jerusalem and thought he could see a cleansing, healing tide of water flowing out of the restored Temple in such abundance that it could be swam in. Can you imaging these waters flowing out from here to the farthest reaches of the earth to heal and soothe the whole world? If so, then I'll bet you can see them returning like a mighty flood, to wash us again, to water and refresh us, to ordain us to ministry, to flow in our veins, and to carry us out to a thirsty world to give all God's people to drink.

GOD'S LOVE WILL BRING YOU HOME   SUSAN K. BOCK

MOSES AND THE BURNING BUSH

Moses had this fire in the belly to rescue helpless folks!

Maybe it came from his own precarious start, when first his mother and then the Pharaoh's daughter rescued him from the murderous jealousy and fear of the Pharaoh, who thought there were far too many of those vigorous Hebrews dwelling in Egypt. He couldn't oppress them enough to subdue them, so he ordered that all their boy babies be killed.

After his rescue, Moses grew up in the palace, pampered, protected, and privileged. It was a great life, as you might guess, but it was a borrowed life, and not his own. Here was Moses, Mosheh, the one drawn out of the water, a Hebrew peasant, living like an Egyptian prince! But he knew there was something else, somewhere more, something of his own that was missing, so one day, he went off in search of it, in search of himself.

His search was as innocent and naive as those urges always are, and just as fateful. Because he came upon a Hebrew, one of his own people, being beaten by an Egyptian. He looked around to be sure they were alone, then he killed the Egyptian and hid his body in the sand.

Next day, still in search of his lost self, Moses went out again among the Hebrew people. When he found two of them fighting each other, he got in the middle of that, too, but was rebuffed and derided for his meddling, and that's how he found out the deed was known. Pharaoh knew of the murder and was after him to kill him, so Moses fled to the desert of Midian.

Well, out in the desert, he came to a well where the seven daughters of Midian's priest were trying to water their sheep, but couldn't because some boy shepherds kept harassing them. Moses intervened again. (Note the early, persistent signs of his calling—Moses just can't help himself!)

His reward for helping the damsels in distress was a wife, and then a child, and the Good Life, into which he settled with alarming ease, but, of course the Good Life was all he knew. Soon Moses' life was all planned out again, right through retirement—predictable, peaceful, and secure. It escaped his notice that, once again, it wasn't his own life he was living, but a borrowed one. Somewhere between Egypt and Midian was Moses' real life, Moses' people, Moses' work, but he'd gotten quite good at circling round all that!

Years later, on a day like any other in a year like any other, blessed and lovely because of its ordinariness, a gift so rare and precious that most of us fail to notice, Moses was out keeping his sheep, following an irresistible tug toward the west, and Horeb, the mountain of God.

The sheep were quiet and the sun was high and he was lulled into a sleepy, peaceful, brown-gray sameness, when suddenly, over here in his side vision, he noticed a shock of orange-yellow brightness, like a fire. It *was* fire, a slow, hot, lovely blaze in a bush. And Moses turned aside to see it. He turned. And his life was never, ever again the same.

Imagine! After all that time, all that history, all that dancing around the truth of his own life, and over all that distance, God found Moses and called him to the work he was born for. And there was no job posting, no resume, no degrees or interviews or tests or contracts.

Surely later, with Pharaoh's arrogance and stubbornness, and the frogs and lice and boils and locusts, and the bloody river and the people's grumbling and bickering and the desert's relentless heat, surely he remembered with a stab of longing this pastoral life of sameness, sureness, and peace that had slipped from his grasp forever the moment he turned aside to see, to hear the God who is fire, and whose love, and call, and purpose for each of us, *for each of us*, are like fire.

Even Moses. Timid, ordinary, hot-headed. Plus, he lisped. And was hopelessly drawn to comfort and ease! So why him? Why him instead of some more believable, articulate, charismatic Israelite who was already on the scene? That's what he said, too. *Why me, Lord? Who am I to go and do this? Who am I?*

We might wonder, too. And wonder, as well, why Peter, bumbling and cowardly? Why Mary, dirt-poor and powerless? Why Paul, arrogant and strong-willed? Why David, lascivious and immature? Why Joseph, spoiled and haughty? Why Sarah, old and irreverent? Why you? Why me? Why this thing to do? Why now? Who could say?

All we can know is that each of us is called by fire, into fire. A fiery ordeal, a fire in the belly, a burning passion. A fiery God calls us to the fire, and into and through and beyond the fire. And why?

Because he hears the cries of his people, and he sees their affliction, and comes down to save them, and needs our help to do it. And if you're going to rescue folks from the fires of affliction and sorrow and wandering and brokenness and ignorance of the God who loves them, you have to get in the fire with them. That's how God called Moses, and in some hot, bright way that you can't ignore, will surely call you, too.

THE MAN BORN BLIND

His world is small and dark, the man born blind, just a tiny plot of ground where he sits every day, inside the gates of the city, his water jar here, his begging bowl there, some food and a mat, perhaps, tucked safely at his side.

When Jesus walks by he doesn't really see him. Not until the disciples turn the man into a problem, an object of debate, but then, seeing someone in need, Jesus throws himself, as always, body and soul, into making it right. He can't be bothered with blame and guilt.

Using spit, believed in his day to have curative power, he makes a small lump of clay, molds it tenderly into the cavities where the useless eyes are set, and sends the man off to a pond called Siloam to wash and be healed. And the man, who's never been able to do much of anything for himself, washes away his own blindness, restoring his sight with his own touch!

Now, the first thing the once-blind man sees are the brilliant, clear blue waters in the pond, and then the thousand shades of green all around, dotted with wildflowers, and then stones and rocks in their endless variety lining the road back to town. But then he notices the brown sameness of the buildings ahead, and the ghetto dwellings of the poor, and the people—tall, short, fat, thin, brown, browner. And then the beggars he'd sat beside, and their blank, hungry stares, and his old neighbors, who seeing him seeing, aren't sure what they see. And, finally, some Pharisees, their faces twisted in anger and fear, who engage him in a long, tiresome contest before they finally expel him from the Temple.

He sees it all. He sees it *all,* and begins to wonder if sight is worth it—maybe blindness wasn't really so bad! His hearing, back then, was extraordinary, and no one expected anything of him. No one would have bothered with his opinion when he was blind and poor. True, he couldn't see children at play, but neither could he see them suffering and abused. He couldn't see the beautiful face of a woman he loved, but neither did he have to watch that face grow tired and old. He couldn't see the beauty of the Temple, but neither did he have to see the squalor of poverty.

Jesus finds him and says, "So. Now you've seen it all, the best and the worst. And how has your heart fared? What's it like to see? To really see? And can you still believe?"

Wary and wiser now, the man asks, "What, sir, should I believe?"

"Well," says Jesus, "see me seeing you with love, and know that God has come near to you."

And seeing that he'll need this God, this love, to keep his eyes open, he throws his heart open, too, and calling him now not "Sir" but "Lord," he falls at his feet and declares his belief.

Meanwhile, the Pharisees have gone sort of blind, their vision narrowing until all they can see in the very goodness that is shining all around them is evil and sin, a cause for fear.

There is told a Sufi story about a man bent over on hands and knees at the market, looking for his house keys. A friend happens by and joins him on all fours to help with the search. Finally the friend asks, "Where exactly did you last see your keys?" The man replies, "In my house." "Then why," asks the friend, "are we looking out here?" "Because," says the man, "it's too dark in the house."

Jesus finds us sitting in all the shadowy darkness of our own lives and souls, making do, pretending to see, and shines a light that heals and opens wide our eyes, a light that helps us refuse the darkness and see with his seeing, a light that softly awakens us to his constant presence, and keeps our hearts warm, and open, and soft.

Then he leads us into a dark and hurting world and, through us, shines a light there, that we might see and love all that he sees and loves.

Open our eyes, Lord, and the eyes of our hearts, and help us to see, really see.

THE PRODIGAL SON

Imagine.

Imagine the despair...the boredom...the emptiness inside...a darkness so dark that he wanted his father dead.

When he went to his father and said, "I want my share of the inheritance, and I want it now," it was the same as saying, "You are dead to me," for it was only when a father lay dying and breathing his last that he bestowed his blessing and his wealth.

It crushed him, this father, and now he wished he *were* dead. And all of the pleading of those who still loved him could not begin to mend his grief.

"You still have great wealth!" said his servants.

"You still have my love," said his wife.

"You still have me, Father," said his other son.

And, indeed, it was, in the end, only *that* which kept him alive. For he loved each of them as though there were just one of them. The father loved each child as though there *were* just *one* child.

Each of them was reason enough to rise and greet the morning sun. Each of them held in his own two hands the father's whole heart. He felt so tenderly toward them, so vulnerable. Whatever was he *thinking*, bringing children into this world?!

Well, he wasn't thinking at all, of course. It was love that brought them here, and love, one way or another, always breaks your heart.

He wondered so often about his young son. What he was doing, where he was. He prayed that the boy was happy and safe. His whole life this child had been possessed of a yearning and longing, and he...well, he would've given his very own life to fill it.

But this son had been determined to go his own way. Even if it killed him. Even if it killed them all.

Meanwhile, the young son was off in a strange and distant place, trying all the things he had once dreamed would fill him. Wine, women, and song. Transcendental meditation and yoga. A membership at the local fitness club. That he'd run out of money wasn't even the worst of it. It was that he'd run out of things to try, things to hide in and numb himself with. The worst of it was that he'd come to the end of himself, and nothing is worse than coming to the end of yourself.

He longed for someone to find him there. He missed his father so much it hurt, making it hard to breathe. But he couldn't admit that, not even to himself, and so he threw himself unreservedly into his pathetic and hungry search, until he awoke one morning with his face in a gutter, his head splitting, his clothes dirty and wet.

He'd truly come to the end of himself. But it was the only place, the *only* place, to start over. So he picked himself up and turned toward home.

Thank heaven my father is more merciful than just, he thought. But how can I face him? How can I ever face him after this terrible and killing thing that I have done? I will beg him to let me serve him as a slave. At least I will be safe, and fed. At least I will be near him again.

The father had seen the child return a million times, in his dreams, in distant mirages. But this time, the mirage didn't fade. His heart skipped a beat.

"Don't trifle with me, God," he warned the Almighty.

Then he began to walk toward the vision. Then, to run, and shout, and laugh!

Now, I can't begin to tell you what it was like when they finally reached each other. The trembling old hands covering the young wet cheeks, the weeping and laughing and tumble of words. But you probably know deep down in your heart. Haven't you found … haven't you *been* found, just like that?

In the wild party that followed, the father basked in the warmth of this gift returned. To receive something back, once lost, so dear, is like stepping out of hell, like getting a second birth.

The other son, at first, was jealous and angry. But he was able to talk about it to his father, so he wouldn't need a lot of expensive therapy later on. And the father led him into the party because it wasn't a party at all, he said, unless both of his children were there. And, finally, all was well.

The father spent the rest of his days just watching his children, holding them near and dear in his gaze, and wondering at the goodness of God.

And the sons? Well, they grew up, drenched in love, like weeds doused in sunshine, side by side, tall, good, and content.

THE STATIONS OF THE CROSS FOR CHILDREN

This is a script for a meditation for children, either gathered on the floor, or walking from station to station. Any of the following props may be used and passed around so that children can feel, smell, and taste the story. Needed are: charoset (chopped apples, honey, and cinnamon), parsley, and salt water (Seder foods); a chalice and wine, flatbread, a bowl with oiled water; rough jute rope, rich purple fabric; a crown of thorns; a large bowl with water for Pilate; nails; Veronika's veil (gauzy fabric with a face vaguely chalked on it); a sponge with vinegar; cotton balls with fragrant oil; linen. Music for "Dayenu" can be found online.

If you wanted to celebrate the beginning of our nation, where would you go to do it? *(Elicit answers: Boston, perhaps, or Philadelphia, or Washington, D.C.)*

And how would you celebrate? *(Probably with parades, fireworks, food for sure!)*

In Jesus' time, where do you think the Jewish people went to celebrate their liberation? *(To the city of Jerusalem.)*

And do you know the name of the holiday that still marks their freedom? *(It is called Passover.)*

When Jesus lived, all the people would go up to Jerusalem for Passover. There they sang and danced and prayed and ate! At the Seder meal, they would tell their children the story of how God had saved them from slavery in Egypt. "Why is this night different from all other nights?" the children would ask. "On this night, God opened the Red Sea waters and the Jewish people passed through the sea on dry ground, but the Egyptians who chased them drowned in the sea!"

"Why do we eat *charoset?*" the children would ask. "Because of the mortar for the bricks our mothers and fathers had to make in their hard labor in Egypt!"

"Why do we eat bitter herbs dipped in salt?" the children would ask. "Because of the bitterness and tears of our slavery!"

"Why do we eat unleavened bread?" the children would ask. "Because there was no time to wait for the bread to rise the night we escaped from Egypt!"

Every spring, from the time Jesus was a boy, the Jewish people have gathered at Passover meals to tell that same story with the children. They say, "Next year, may we celebrate this meal in Israel, our home!"

They sing: "Da da ye nu, da da ye nu, da da ye nu, dayenu, dayenu!" *(It would have been enough for us!)*

> If God had split the sea for us, *Dayenu!*
> If God had sustained us in the wilderness for forty years, *Dayenu!*
> If God had brought us before Mount Sinai, *Dayenu!*
> If God had given us the Torah, *Dayenu!*
> If God had led us to the land of Israel, *Dayenu!*

In Jesus' time, the people waited for a king to come and free them from the Romans who ruled over them in their own homeland. This king would come at Passover, entering the holy city riding on a colt. He would be like a god, able to heal blindness and do other miracles. So, when Jesus came onto Jerusalem on a colt, many thought he was the Messiah, and they made a huge parade, and shouted "Hosanna! Hosanna!" They made a path with their palms and their clothes. The children sang the loudest, and when people tried to quiet them, Jesus said, "If you silence them, the stones will start to sing!"

The people thought that Jesus would lead them into a great war, a war they could win, and that after all these years they would be free at last! But there was no war, and the people became sad, scared, and angry. The same people who had welcomed him with such joy and love began to want to kill Jesus.

Jesus knew what was happening. He knew the people wanted him dead. He was sad, scared, and angry, too, because he had thought things would surely turn out differently than this. But he trusted God, and listened to God every minute so that he would know what to do next.

Jesus gathered his friends in a small room and they shared their last meal together. As always, he blessed the bread and the wine, but this time he said something different. He said, "From now on, when you eat or drink like this, remember how I loved you, and know that I am with you."

After supper, Jesus got up from the table and washed his friends' feet, to show them how they ought to serve each other.

Here, the children may share bread and wine, and pass the bowl of oiled water around to smell and feel. You may want to do a real foot-washing, while a simple song is sung.

One of Jesus' closest friends, Judas, was so angry that he left and told the police where to find Jesus so they could arrest him. The police paid Judas thirty pieces of silver for this information. Later, when Judas looked at his money and counted it, he realized that no amount of money is worth your love and loyalty.

In the garden of Gethsemane, Jesus was praying, and Roman soldiers came to arrest him. They tied his hands together, like a criminal, though Jesus had never used his hands to hit or hurt anyone, but only to heal and soothe. The soldiers dressed him in a fancy purple robe, and a crown that they made of thorns.

These items may be passed around.

They blindfolded him, and spat at him, and beat him, and shouted, "Some king you are! If you're a prophet, then tell us who just hit you!"

They took him to Pilate, who really wanted to know the truth about things. He said to Jesus, "Who are you?" Jesus was silent. Jesus knew that what was happening to him was not fair, and that, if he spoke, he might be able to save himself. But sometimes we need to be silent and he knew this was one of those times. Pilate washed his hands in a bowl of water in front of all the people as a sign that he would not be guilty for whatever might happen to Jesus.

Jesus was led to a hill. He was made to carry his own cross. He was so tired and hungry and sad that he had trouble carrying it. Many people gathered to watch the spectacle. Some made fun of him, some wept, and some helped him, like Veronika.

The legend of Veronika is that the image of Jesus' face remained on her veil when, breaking with tradition and safety, she ran to him, removed her veil, and wiped his face.

Simon helped him carry his cross. They nailed Jesus to a cross, and his life slipped slowly away from him. He wondered why this was happening to him, and where his God was now that he needed God more than ever. He became very thirsty, so some soldiers held up a vinegar-soaked sponge for him to suck on.

The sponge with vinegar may be passed around.

Just before he died, Jesus gathered up his last little bit of strength and shouted to God in the saddest, loudest cry anyone ever heard. And he died.

He was taken down from the cross and wrapped in white linen. Then he was put in a small cave for a tomb, and a huge stone was rolled in front of it. The next day, some women came with oil and spices to anoint Jesus' body.

The oil-soaked cotton and piece of linen may be passed around.

Only, when they got there, they found that the body was gone! They were angry and confused and ran to tell Peter and the others what they had discovered.

This is a Holy Week story, whose end comes at Easter. I wonder how the story will turn out.

EASTER

Make us an Easter people,
O Christ, whose name
is "Alleluia."

May we, like Mary,
rise in joy when you call our name.
May we, like Thomas,
see and believe.
May we, like Peter,
become bold and brave.
May we, like Cleopas,
meet you in every road.

May we, like them,
be utterly changed,
in the victory of the love
by which you left your tomb,
and saved us forever
from death.

In your name, Jesus.
Amen.

An Affirmation of Faith for the Easter Season

Alleluia, we believe!
And, believing, we sing "Alleluia!"

In the God of life and goodness,
In the Christ who brings us home,
In the Spirit who comforts and keeps us,
Alleluia, we believe!
And, believing, we sing "Alleluia!"

In our many gifts for serving,
In the call of each disciple,
In the church whose work is love,
Alleluia, we believe!
And, believing, we sing "Alleluia!"

In the saints who pray for us,
In the scriptures that bring us truth,
In the sacraments that give grace,
Alleluia, we believe!
And, believing, we sing "Alleluia!"

In the hope of resurrection,
In the rising to eternal life,
In the dawning of God's reign,
Alleluia, we believe!
And, believing, we sing "Alleluia!"

May we ever be true to all we believe,
And our song ever be "Alleluia!"
Amen.

The Prayers of the People for the Easter Season

Awake, O Sleeper, rise from death,
And Christ will give you life!

Bring newness and change to your church, O God,
that we might serve you with courage and grace.
Awake, O Church, rise from death,
And Christ will give you life!

Bring newness and change to your world, O God,
that all might know the goodness of your love.
Awake, O World, rise from death,
And Christ will give you life!

Bring newness and change to our nation, O God,
that each person might share and honor the other.
Awake, O People, rise from death,
And Christ will give you life!

Bring newness and change for the suffering, O God,
that they might know your saving help.
Awake, O Sorrowful, rise from death,
And Christ will give you life!

Bring newness and change to even the departed, O God,
that they might forever grow in your likeness.
Awake, O Saints, rise from death,
And Christ will give you life!

Bring newness and change to our hearts, O God,
that we might grow larger in faith and hope.
Awake, O Soul, rise from death,
And Christ will give you life!

The people pray their particular concerns and thanksgivings.

Awake, O Sleeper, rise from death, for Christ has burst forth from the tomb, making all things new. Rise and live, says the Lord. This day God has made for life and all joy! Amen, alleluia!
Alleluia, amen!

CREATION

A Poem

This story, which is featured in Caroline Fairless's audio recording of biblical stories, is read with a drumbeat "behind" the words. The rhythm, volume, and tempo can change anywhere, as the drummer responds to the words. Each time the reader says "so good," the congregation echoes it.

In the beginning, there was nothing but water,
deep and cold, deep and cold,
with a blanket of darkness stretched all across,
and a wind moaning over it all.
In the beginning, before God spoke,
there was only this dark, cold void.

Let there be light! God said, and there was,
and it was . . . so good! *(So good!)*
The light split the night, and the first day was made.
And a dome, that God called "Sky,"
to hold the waters, safe in their places,
above and below, so good! *(So good!)*

By God's command, there appeared dry land,
to push the waters together.
The land was called Earth, the waters were Seas,
and strolling the shores, God was pleased.

Then God told the Earth to put forth seeds,
and plants and fruits and trees.
And she did! She turned the whole world green,
and juicy, and fragrant, and moist.

On the fourth day, God spoke to the Sky,
and called for a Sun to rule the day,
and a Moon to gently guard the night.
And stars were set shining,
and shooting and falling,

for guiding and gazing.
And it all was so good! *(So good!)*

Let there be creatures! said God, that fly
and swim and lumber and crawl,
and there were, and it was...so good. *(So good!)*
So God blessed them, blessed them all,
saying, Fill up the Earth, and the Sky, and the Seas!
And they did. God was pleased.
Then God said, Let us make people,
in the image of Us! In our likeness, a woman and man.
They shall be stewards of all this creation,
and they shall make children,
whose children make children,
and good it shall be, so good! *(So good!)*

So God spoke, and blew breath,
and people were made,
and given the care of the Earth
which God said would feed them.
And God blessed them, it pleased him.
God smiled at the goodness. So good! *(So good!)*

God saw all that had come to be,
and was pleased at the land and sky and sea,
And the life that they swarmed with,
and the noise it all made,
and the color and rhythm and song.

So God sat down for a well-deserved rest,
and with a contented sigh,
and a heart full of pleasure,
said, This is so good! *(So good!)*
This is so very, very good!
This is so good! *(So good!)*

CREATION

A Congregational Reading

In the beginning, on the first day, God created the heavens and the earth. God said, "Let there be light" and there was light. And God saw that is was good.
Blessed be the God of Light.

In the beginning, on the second day, God created a dome to separate the waters from the waters. God called the dome sky, and saw that it was good.
Blessed be the God of Waters and Sky.

In the beginning, on the third day, God gathered the waters together and let dry land appear. God spoke, and the earth brought forth every color of green, and God saw that it was good.
Blessed be the God of Green-Brown Earth.

In the beginning, on the fourth day, God created the sun, the moon and the stars, to separate day from night, to mark the seasons. And God saw that it was good.
Blessed be the God of the Heavens and of Time.

In the beginning, on the fifth day, God created all the living creatures of sea and sky, and blessed them, and called them good.
Blessed be the God of Wing and Flight, of Soaring and Swimming.

In the beginning, on the sixth day, God created the animals of the earth, and made humankind in the image of God, and God saw it was very good.
Blessed be the God of our Hearts, the God of Flesh and Souls and Loving.

In the beginning, on the seventh day, God created rest, and entered into a rest from all the work that had been done. And God saw that rest was very, very good, indeed.
Blessed be the God of Holy Rest and Play.

These verses can be added when used at times other than the Easter Vigil:

In the unfolding of time, God chose a people to help make known to all the world the breadth and depth of the divine love.
Blessed be the God who remembered this beloved world with longing and tenderness.

In the unfolding of time, God heard the cries of a people in bondage, and led them out, through wilderness, to a home of abundance.

Blessed be the God who liberates, and prepares a home for us all in his love.

In the unfolding of time, God spoke through prophets, calling for goodness and truth.

Blessed be the God whose voice is never silent, who may ever be heard and obeyed.

In the unfolding of time, God laid a straight and level path, strewn with blossoms, and traversing streams of water.

Blessed be the God who finds us in exile, and restores us in safety and belonging.

In the fullness of time, God gave us Jesus, who proclaimed a new covenant and in whose likeness we are made and called.

Blessed be the God Incarnate, who worked and played, rested and loved, who laughed and wept and dreamed.

In the fullness of time, God gave us the Spirit, who stays with us always to guide and bless.

Blessed be God, our God, whose love creates and calls, heals and mends, blesses and sends. Blessed be our God, forever and ever. Amen.

ADAM AND EVE'S REBELLION

A Simple Skit

Needed are a Narrator, a Serpent, Adam, Eve, and God. Our "God" was played by a gentle young girl, who wore big sunglasses and sat on a lounge chair filing her nails, and it was wonderful!

Narrator	Now, the serpent was more sneaky than any other creature that God had made. The serpent said to the woman:
Serpent	Did God s-s-s-s-s-say, "You mus-s-s-s-tn't eat of any tree in the garden?"
Eve	We may eat the fruit of every tree, God said, except for the fruit of the tree in the middle of the garden. If you even touch that fruit, you will die!"
Serpent	*(very sarcastically)* You will not die! You s-s-s-see, God knows that when you eat it, your eyes-s-s-s-s will be opened, and you will be like God, knowing what is good from what is evil.
Narrator	So Eve looked again, and decided that the fruit looked very beautiful, and delicious, and since it would make a person wise, she took the fruit and ate it. Then she gave some to her husband and he ate it, too.
	Suddenly, they saw things differently, and knew they were naked, and were embarrassed. They took fig leaves and sewed them into aprons. Then they heard the sound of the Lord God walking in the garden in the cool of the day, and they hid from God among the trees.
God	*(with tenderness)* Where are you?
Adam	I heard you walking in the garden, and I was afraid, because I was naked. So I hid.
God	Who told you that you were naked? Did you eat the fruit that I told you not to eat?
Adam	That woman that you gave to be with me, she gave me the fruit to eat!

God	*(sadly)* What have you done?
Eve	The serpent tricked me, and I ate the fruit.
Narrator	And so, God punished the serpent, saying:
God	Because you did this, from now on, you shall crawl on your belly, and eat dust all your days. And you and the people shall be enemies. You shall bruise their heel, and they shall bruise your head.

All the actors sadly part from each other, each going a different direction to leave the "stage."

Noah and the Flood

A Dramatic Reading

Needed are a Reader, Noah, and God.

Reader   God's heart was breaking, because God's people had forgotten the love for which they were made. God was angrier and sadder than God ever got. When God looked down on the earth, God saw that Noah, alone, was a good person. So God said:

God   Noah, build an ark!

Noah   Sure, Lord! . . . Uh, what's an ark?

God   It's a huge boat, like this long . . .

Reader   And God stretched out his arms as far as they would go. *(With his arms, God demonstrates in each direction.)*

God   and this wide, and this tall.

Reader   And God reached up into the heavens as far as his arms would reach. Then God said:

God   When it's finished, go into the boat, with your wife, and your children, and your grandchildren, and shut the door tight.

Noah   Cool! Like a cruise. I've always wanted to go on a cruise.

Reader   "Well," said God, "not exactly."

God   You see, it's going to rain and rain, so there won't be any sunbathing. And no moonlit dances on the deck to the sounds of a big band.

Reader   And Noah said,

Noah   Oh.

Reader   "And one more thing," said God.

God	You'll be taking some animals with you.
Noah	Well, sure. Like my dog Skip and my cat Fluffy?
God	Yeah, and a few others. Noah, I am going to send a flood, and all the earth will die, so I want you to take with you, into the ark, a *he* and a *she* of every kind of living thing. A *he* and a *she* of every animal, a *he* and a *she* of every bird, and a *he* and a *she* of every reptile. So that when you come out of the ark, every kind of life may begin again.
Reader	And all this happened when Noah was six hundred years old, which just goes to show you that, even when you're very old, God may find you and ask you to do something brave. So Noah built the ark, and gathered the animals, and went into the ark, and slammed the door...! And just as he was wondering,
Noah	Oh, my, what have I done?
Reader	the rain began, soft at first, and then louder and louder, and the thunder rolled and the lightning flashed. They couldn't see it, but they could tell by the way the ark rocked and pitched and rolled. In the ark it was noisy, and smelly, and everyone was very afraid, and more than a little bit sick to their stomachs.
Noah	I don't feel so good....
Reader	The rain fell upon the earth for forty days and forty nights. And then it began to let up, and finally it stopped altogether, and the ark came to rock gently on the waves of the great sea that covered all the earth. Noah sent a dove out the window, and it flew everywhere looking for someplace to land, but it couldn't find even a treetop. He waited seven days, and sent her out again, but this time she returned with a fresh olive branch in her beak, so Noah knew the water was going down, down, ever so slowly down. So then everyone rested, and waited. Finally, Noah and his wife and their children and grandchildren, and all the animals and birds and reptiles left the ark. And as they walked out, the mud squished up between their toes...
Noah	and we looked up and saw the sky filled with rainbows, and we heard God's voice, weak with sorrow and regret, saying:
God	Never again. This is my promise: Never again.
Reader	"Whenever you see the rainbow," said God,
God	remember my promise. My love is too great to ever again do harm to my creation. My promise from now till forever is a love that will keep you safe, and hold you close to my heart.

THE QUARRY SONG

SUSAN K. BOCK

THE ESCAPE FROM EGYPT

Needed are two small groups of actors, Moses, a Reader, and God's voice. The Reader may rehearse with worshipers who will prepare to blow gently while Moses' hand is outstretched and stop blowing when his hand is dropped.

As the reader begins, the "Israelites," with Moses at their head, are wandering up the aisle, looking up and around in awe at the pillars of cloud and fire, pointing, whispering, etc.

Meanwhile, the "Red Sea" is in place at the sanctuary, facing each other in two lines and making water and waves, with fabric, or their arms, or however they best think to do it!

Reader	When the Jewish people left Egypt, the Lord went in front of them in a pillar of cloud by day, and in a pillar of fire by night. Neither the pillar of cloud nor the pillar of fire left its place in front of the people. As Pharaoh drew near, the Israelites looked back and saw the Egyptians chasing them. They cried to the Lord, and complained to Moses,
People	*(whining, weeping, and wailing!)* Were there no graves in Egypt, that you have brought us out to die in the wilderness?! Didn't we tell you it would be better for us to stay and be slaves to the Egyptians?
Moses	Do not be afraid, be still, stand firm, and see how the Lord delivers you. You will never see the Egyptians again!

The Israelites turn around, watch, and freeze in various postures of terror, pointing, shivering, etc. Moses listens, upward.

Reader	The Lord said to Moses,
God	Tell the Israelites to go forward. Lift up your staff, stretch out your hand over the sea and divide it, and they will go into the sea on dry ground. I will harden the hearts of the Egyptians, and when they go in after the Israelites I will defeat Pharaoh and his army, and all will know that I am the Lord.

The people turn around and cautiously begin moving forward again.

Reader   Then the angel of the Lord and the pillar of cloud took their place behind the people, to come between the Israelites and the Egyptians, and they were there lighting the night as long as it lasted.

Moses   And, when I stretched out my hand, a strong wind, the whole night long, blew back the sea and formed a wall on either side of the people. We went through the sea on dry land, and the Egyptians followed us.

The Red Sea separates to make room for the people, who move through it.

Reader   In the morning, the Lord in the fire and cloud looked down and threw the Egyptians into a panic, which clogged their chariot wheels. "Let us flee," they said, "for the Lord is on their side!"

The people stand safely on the shore (sanctuary steps) and watch the drama.

Moses   But I stretched out my hand again, and the sea returned to its depth, and the Lord tossed Pharaoh's army into the sea!

The Israelites are rejoicing, dancing, and "high-fiving."

Reader   This is how the Lord saved Israel that day. And they feared the Lord, and believed in his servant, Moses. Then Moses and all the people sang and danced before the Lord, saying,

People   The Lord has triumphed gloriously; he has thrown the horse and its rider into the sea!

The Story of the Escape Through the Red Sea

Reader 1	Why is this night different from all other nights?
People	**This is the Passover of the Lord, when God led us out of slavery in Egypt, through the Red Sea, onto dry ground. We remember...**
Reader 2	how we were slaves for four hundred years in Egypt, where we were treated harshly.
People	**We cried out to the Lord and he heard us, and sent our Father Moses to deliver us!**
Reader 1	God said to Moses "Tell old Pharaoh...
People	**Let my people go!"**
Moses	I was so afraid. I didn't know how to speak to Pharaoh, and how to prove God had sent me. So God sent plagues upon the Egyptians to make his point! There were frogs, and lice, and flies.
People	**There were boils, and hail, and locusts, and there was a darkness so heavy it could be felt!**
Reader 2	Then came the worst and saddest plague of all, the death of every firstborn in all of Egypt land.
Moses	God said, "Have the people eat their last meal in Egypt. Tell them to take one lamb for every family and roast it, and eat it in haste."
People	**We ate it with unleavened bread and bitter herbs, with our sandals on our feet and our walking sticks in our hands. We remember...**
Reader 1	how we took the blood of the lamb and smeared it on our doorposts, so the angel of death would pass over our homes.
Reader 2	And then we rose up and left the land of our oppression! We left so quickly...

People	**our dough was still rising, our kneading bowls were wrapped on our shoulders, our sleeping children were nestled in our arms! We remember...**
Reader 1	how happy we were...until we came to the shores of the sea! And then, of course, we forgot how God had brought us this far, and we began to weep, and wail, and whine! We said...
People	**Were there no graves in Egypt, Moses, that you brought us out here to die? We should never have left! Better to live as slaves than to die in freedom!**
Moses	Imagine being so afraid that you'd rather be slaves to, well, anything, no matter how bad it is! But God said:
Reader 2	"Moses! Tell the people, 'Do not be afraid! Stand firm! For you will never see these Egyptians again. The Lord will fight for you and you have only to stand firm!'"
Reader 1	"Lift up your staff, Moses, and stretch out your hand over the sea and divide it, and the Israelites will go through on dry ground!"
People	**The Lord drove back the sea with a strong east wind that blew all night, and turned the sea to dry land! We remember...**
Moses	how the pillar of cloud went before us and behind us, and when Pharaoh's army came after us, at the morning watch, the Lord looked down and threw them into panic! God said:
Reader 2	"Moses, stretch out your hand again so the waters of the sea may return to their place."
Moses	So I did, and Pharaoh's army was drowned in the sea.
People	**Then we feared the Lord, and believed in his servant Moses!**
Moses	And when we came safely to the shore, we remember how our mothers danced and sang, all through the night...
People	**because God had brought us out of slavery and led us through the sea, to bring us home to the land of promise.**
Readers	It is the Passover of the Lord...
People	**and we remember!**

The Three Hebrew Children in the Fiery Furnace

The reader will rehearse the congregation before the reading.

One side (or one group) learns to say, on this cue: the satraps, the governors,

the counselors, the justices, the magistrates,

The other side learns to say, on this cue: the horn,

the pipe, the harp, and the drum,

*The whole congregation practices saying, on this **and only this** cue:* the golden statue that King Nebuchadnezzar had set up,

Boooo!

And when they hear these words:

for there is no other God who is mighty like this God!

they should cheer, shout "hurrah," applaud, whistle, etc.

The story begins!

King Nebuchadnezzar made a huge golden statue, and set it up in Babylon for all to see. Then he sent for *the satraps, the governors,*

the counselors, the justices, the magistrates,

and all the officials, to come to the dedication of the statue that he had set up. So, *the satraps, the governors,*

the counselors, the justices, the magistrates,

and all the officials came for the dedication of *the golden statue that King Nebuchadnezzar had set up.*

Boooo!

As they stood and looked at it, the herald proclaimed aloud: "You are commanded, O peoples, nations, and languages, that when you hear *the horn,*

the pipe, the harp, and the drum,

and the entire musical ensemble, you are to fall down and worship *the golden statue that King Nebuchadnezzar has set up.*

Boooo!

Whoever does not fall down and worship shall immediately be thrown into a furnace of blazing fire!" And so, as soon as all the peoples heard the sound of *the horn,*

the pipe, the harp, and the drum,

and the entire musical ensemble, all the peoples, nations, and languages fell down and worshiped *the golden statue that King Nebuchadnezzar had set up.*

Boooo!

Now there were certain folks who accused the Jews. They said to the King: "O King, live forever! You, O King, have made a decree, that everyone who hears the sound of *the horn,*

the pipe, the harp, and the drum,

and the entire musical ensemble shall fall down and worship the golden statue, and whoever does not shall be thrown into a furnace of blazing fire. Now, we don't like to tattle, but there are certain Jews, named Shadrach, Meshach, and Abednego, who pay no heed to you, O King. They do not serve your gods and they do not worship your golden statue."

Then Nebuchadnezzar, in a furious rage, commanded that Shadrach, Meshach, and Abednego be brought to him. And the King said, "Is it true, O Shadrach, Meshach, and Abednego, that you do not serve my gods and you do not worship my golden statue? Well, I'm gonna give you one more chance. If, when you hear the sound of *the horn,*

the pipe, the harp, and the drum,

and the entire musical ensemble, you fall down and worship my golden statue, well and good. But if you do not worship, you shall be thrown into a furnace of blazing fire. And who is the god that will deliver you?!"

But Shadrach, Meshach, and Abednego, answered the king, "O Nebuchadnezzar, we don't need to defend ourselves! If our God is able to deliver us, then let him. *For there is no other God who is mighty like this God!*"

(Cheers, "hurrahs," applause, whistles, etc.)

"But if not, you should know, O King, that we will not serve your gods and we will not worship that golden statue!"

Then the king was so mad that his face was twisted! So he ordered that the furnace be heated up seven times hotter than usual, and ordered the strongest guards to bind Shadrach, Meshach, and Abednego and throw them into the furnace of blazing fire.

And the fire was so hot that the raging flames killed the men who threw them in! King Nebuchadnezzar was watching, and was astonished, and said to his counselors, "Wasn't it three men who were bound and thrown into the fire?" They answered, "True, O King."

The king replied, "But I see four men, unbound, walking in the middle of the fire, and they aren't hurt at all, and the fourth one looks like a god!"

King Nebuchadnezzar went to the door of the furnace of blazing fire and said, "Shadrach, Meshach, and Abednego, servants of the Most High God, come out here!"

So, Shadrach, Meshach, and Abednego came out of the fire. And *the satraps, the governors,*

the counselors, the justices, the magistrates,

and all the officials gathered together and saw that the fire had no power over the bodies of these three holy children; their hair was not singed, their clothes were not burned, and not even the smell of fire came from them!

King Nebuchadnezzar said, "Blessed be the God of Shadrach, Meshach, and Abednego, who has sent an angel to delivered the servants who trusted in God. They disobeyed the king's command and yielded up their bodies rather than serve and worship any god but their own God. Therefore, I make a decree:

Any people, nation, or language that utters a word against the God of Shadrach, Meshach, and Abednego shall be torn limb from limb, and their houses laid in ruins. *For there is no other God who is mighty like this God!*"

(Cheers, "hurrahs," applause, whistles, etc.)

EZEKIEL AND THE VALLEY OF DRY BONES

There are two voices, Ezekiel's and God's. There should be people with rattling instruments positioned around the nave, and prepared to add their sound as cued.

Ezekiel   I thought valleys were green and lush, full of sheep and streams and lots of peace. Not this one! One day the Spirit swooped me up and then set me down in the middle of a valley full of bones! God made me walk all through them. There were thousands of them, and they were dry and dead as can be. God asked me:

God   Ezekiel, do you think these bones can live and breathe again?

Ezekiel   And I'm thinking, is this a real question?! Heck no, they can't live. That would be impossible, even for you, Lord. But all I said was, "Uh, what do you think, Lord?"

God   Prophesy to the bones, Ezekiel. Say. . . .

Ezekiel   Wait just a minute! Hold it right there. I'm supposed to talk to this pile of bones? I'm a prophet. I already get grief from everyone. They'll think I've lost it! I'll never live it down. "Well," says God,

God   it might be easier to talk to a pile of bones than to those stubborn people of mine.

Ezekiel   You've got a point, I say. But Lord, this is one of the weirdest things you've ever asked me to do. "As I was saying," says God,

God   Tell this to the bones: Listen up, you dry bones! It's me, God, and I'm going to bring you back from your dry, brittle deadness. I will make you *live* again! I will clothe you with muscle, and flesh, and skin. And then I will breathe over you, and you will live, and you will know that I am your God.

Ezekiel   Well, no one was looking, so I did it. I told the bones just what God said,

The bones begin shaking, working to a crescendo.

and those bones started rattling and shaking and making all kinds of noise, coming together into whole skeletons, covered with muscle and skin, and soon they were whole, new bodies!

But then they just lay there, dead as can be, and it was quiet as a graveyard.

There's a sudden silencing of the rattles and then a pause.

Now see? That's what's wrong with this line of work! God says, "Do this, say that, and it will come to pass and the people will know you're a prophet." Well, I'm still waitin' on about half of those things. For which I was about to give God a piece of my mind when God says,

God   Call the breath, Ezekiel! Call the Spirit! Say, "Come from the four winds, O Breath, and breathe on these bones, that they might live!"

Ezekiel   So I called the breath, and it came! The breath of the earth filled those bones with life and there were too many to count! And then God says: "Ezekiel, my people are like these bones. They are all dried up, with no hope, no future. So tell them, tell my people…"

God   that I will open the graves of their hearts and I will give them spirit, and hope and life, and I will bring them home. And then they will know me, and how I love them, and that I the Lord can bring life even from death, and whatever I say I will do for my people, I can be trusted to do.

I am the Lord.

FIRE!

An Easter Vigil Story

The paschal candle, unlit, is in a prominent place where the story is told.

"All our vanished days are gathered secretly in the memory," said a mystic. Let's see if we can find some of those vanished days.

Long, long ago, our ancient mothers and fathers sat in dark, damp, cold caves, waiting, waiting, for the sun, for spring, in such darkness, such cold. Can you feel it? It makes me shiver to remember!

In the cold they labored over a dry timber for a spark that might, if they were lucky, start a fire, a fire for warmth and for cooking, a fire that was kept always alive, and even carried in a pot from camp to camp. If the fire died, the people could die, too!

Look! A tiny spark has caught. *(The paschal candle is lit.)*

Can you gently blow on it to help it along? Don't blow too hard. Look, it's getting bigger now! Watch the Easter flame until you can bring it inside you and, when you are ready, close your eyes and follow the flame back, back and down, into your memory, back to a campfire. It may have been last summer, or last week, or five years ago, or thirty. Do you remember the fire?

Remember how hot and bright it was, and how you gazed at its flames, transfixed? Remember how the fire had a life of its own, dancing, leaping, hunkering down? Remember how you sometimes talked, or laughed, or sang, and sometimes were silent, entranced? Following the showers of sparks up to the sky, can you see the stars arrange themselves into dippers, warriors, bears?

Now follow your memory way, way back, to Palestine, at a campfire one ancient spring night, where our old mothers and fathers are telling our story to the children. "Remember the Great Flood?" they're saying. "Remember how the waters covered the whole earth, and how smelly it was in that ark, and how good that soggy ground felt when we came out? Remember how the sky was brilliant with rainbows?"

"And remember when we crossed the sea, and the waters stood on end, just for us, and our feet didn't even get wet? Remember how the sea fell down again, just in time, and how our mothers danced and sang all through the night, wild with joy? Remember? Nothing feels as good as freedom! Nothing stirs the blood like a narrow escape. Can you feel it? Do you remember?"

And the children would remember, somewhere deep inside.

Can you remember now? Can you see the waters, the skies? Can you smell the fresh earth? Can you feel the warmth of the fire? Can you see our elders huddled at the fire on cool nights, at home in the Promised Land, laughing, singing, telling the story?

"And remember," they're saying now, "how Shadrach, Meshach, and Abednego walked around in the flames, and, though Nebuchadnezzar had made the furnace seven times hotter, God stood between them and the fire, so they came out without even the smell of smoke on them? Remember?"

And the children would remember, and shudder, a little, to think how close to death they had come in that furnace.

Now follow your memory forward a bit, to the fire where you sat huddled with Peter, cold and afraid, waiting for word, from inside the palace, of your sweet Jesus, and how you heard Peter say, "I told you, I don't know him!" Remember how Peter wept for shame and how you both shivered from the chill on your heart, even as the fire burned your face?

And come forward a bit more to a sandy beach in Palestine, one spring dawn, where you are gathered with others, wet and cold, warming yourself at a fire where fish and bread are cooking. Jesus is serving you breakfast, and nothing tastes as good as a meal served with love, ready and waiting, after a long night of work. Can you taste it, salty, crusty, and hot?

Still gazing into the campfire, follow the flames even further forward to a tiny golden flame on top of a candle, in church. It may be the Easter light, in procession, at the Great Vigil, the only light, in a cool, dark, tomb-like sanctuary. Or it might be a candle at the altar, or a baptismal candle—yours or someone else's. You might be very young, or very middle-aged, or very old. You're in a church, and there's the loveliest music, and you are safe and wanted and loved, and you could just stay here, right here, forever. Do you remember?

Now follow that flame back to this one, here, now. Take a few deep breaths and when you are ready, bring yourself back to tonight and open your eyes.

This is our story, yours and mine, not in some sweet, sentimental, pretending kind of way, but really and truly ours. In telling it, again and again, our vanished days are dusted off, our hearts sit up and listen, and our souls are lighted again with the fire we carry inside, always, like the ancients carried their potted fire. With the fire inside us rekindled, may we leave this place to gather the world into the story and into the love which tells it. Amen.

EASTER MORNING

A Dramatic Reading for Two Women

Needed are actors for Mary (Jesus' mother) and Magdalene. This works well as the very first thing to happen on Easter morning, just preceding a grand opening hymn!

Mary and Magdalene enter from the back of the nave, with Mary scurrying way ahead. They are carrying bottles of oil and pieces of torn linen. In the aisle they begin speaking.

Magdalene	Mary, why are you in such a hurry to get to this sad business?
Mary	And why, Magdalena, are *you* so *slow*?! What has to be done has to be done. Then maybe we can get back to... well, to what we used to call "living"...
Magdalene	*(wistfully)* before he began to speak of things that lit up our days...
Mary	and stole our hearts...
Magdalene	and gave us hope...
Mary	and caused us wonder. How he always made me wonder! What was it that burned inside him? If I hadn't been there, and felt every pain, I would never believe he came from me.

Each is now turning toward the congregation, lost in her own thoughts.

Magdalene	Why would he love me?
Mary	Why couldn't he stay home, like a good Jewish boy, and take care of his mother?
Magdalene	He didn't seem to believe what others had said about me.

Mary	*(Smelling the myrrh, which sobers her.)* Right from the start, nothing made sense. Like those strange travelers from the East bringing useless gifts. Men! *(She smells it again and reflects.)* "To honor a king," they said. As though every child weren't a queen or a prince to its mother! *(There's a reflective pause.)* Too bad such love can't save them.
Magdalene	The thing is, when someone looks at you, and speaks to you, and listens to you, like he can see your heart...like you were *somebody,* well, it makes you think maybe you could live in your own skin after all.
Mary	The damnable thing about it is, I was the one who taught him to follow his heart...
Magdalene	The ancient promises of Torah were mine, too, he said,...
Mary	no matter the cost.
Magdalene	and he needed our friendship as much as I did, I think, to help him do what he did.
Mary	"Always follow your heart," I said, "for what's a life worth, without the courage of love?" *(A pause.)* I guess he was my son, after all.

They return to conversation with each other.

Magdalene	I tore these cloths from my finest piece of linen during the night. Well, I was awake, anyway.
Mary	He would want us to go on, wouldn't he?
Magdalene	I can't believe otherwise.
Mary	I'd rather crawl into that tomb with him.
Magdalene	There's so much he didn't finish. So many he didn't reach.
Mary	Maybe...maybe we could do some of it...
Magdalene	if we helped each other.
Mary	Right now, I'm just working on breathing!

They embrace, and move on, arm in arm.

Mary	C'mon. Let's go.
Magdalene	Mary, how will we ever roll away that huge stone?

THE ROAD TO EMMAUS

A Dramatic Reading for Two People

The actors, Cleopas and his Companion, will walk up the aisle as they read, each talking to the congregation on his or her side. For interest, they can cross paths several times, and change which side they're talking to. When the "meal" begins they should be at the front, turn to face the people, and remain there until, at "headed us back to town," they can start back down the aisle to finish the dialogue.

Cleopas	Have you ever walked the road to Emmaus?
Companion	Have you ever walked along, so numb with grief, you didn't really know or care where your feet might take you?
Cleopas	Have you ever walked the road of heartbreak...
Companion	having fled the scene in fear, just when others needed you most?
Cleopas	Have you ever been on the wrong road?
Companion	Well, then, maybe you know, just a little, how Cleopas and I felt that day we ran away from Jerusalem and headed for Emmaus.
Cleopas	Our feet were like stones. And our senses were so dull, we didn't even notice the wonder of spring, bursting all around us.
Companion	All we could think, or feel, or talk about was how we missed him, how much it hurt...
Cleopas	how awful it was, and wondering how we'd ever go on.
Companion	So we didn't see the stranger, even when he fell in step with us,...
Cleopas	eavesdropping, clearing his throat, kicking stones, humming loudly!

Companion	"What are you two talking about," he says, "and what's got you so sad on the finest spring morning of the world? Did you notice the buds on the trees? And the sun is warmer and brighter than it's ever been, ever!"
Cleopas	But what he meant was, "How could you have hoped to go home again, after all that's happened to you?"
Companion	Well, you always want to go home, even if it wasn't so good. Have you ever tried it, to go back to what you knew, because what you didn't know was just too scary?
Cleopas	But, well, God always calls us away from home, away from what's safe, and familiar...
Companion	or home by a whole other road...
Cleopas	or to some frontier where only faith will do.
Companion	*Only* faith.
Cleopas	And I'd bet he was thinking how he'd told us to meet him in Galilee, which was due north of Jerusalem.
Companion	And Emmaus?
Cleopas	Due east!
Companion	Sometimes, without the courage to stay put, or go forward, we get on some other road, any path but the one we're called to!
Cleopas	But God always finds us, no matter how lost we are, and lovingly turns us back.
Companion	Like the stranger did that day. We thought, at first, he was just another pilgrim returning from Passover in Jerusalem, and we couldn't believe he hadn't heard of the terrible things that had happened there.
Cleopas	So we told him about Jesus.
Companion	How he'd wakened our hearts and lives like a spring morning breeze...
Cleopas	and spoke with the power of truth...
Companion	and touched the loveless with grace...
Cleopas	and rekindled in everyone the hope of messiah!

Companion	We thought he was the one, he *must* be the one, if he could take our small, tattered lives, . . .
Cleopas	and make them count for something good. He must be the messiah! But he wasn't, we told the stranger, because now he's dead.
Companion	And for three long days we have bickered and blamed, trembled and hid, brooded and wept. And then some of the women came from the tomb this morning and said the body was gone!
Cleopas	They'd "seen angels."
Companion	Well, when women start seeing things, and grown men keep crying, you have to do something.
Cleopas	So we went to see for ourselves.
Companion	The tomb was empty, all right, but that was all. So I said to Cleopas, I can't stay here anymore. This city is crazy and dangerous, and just too sad.
Cleopas	The stranger listened and listened, like a person should do when they want to help you back from grief, and he coaxed our hearts, oh-so-gently, back to life . . .
Companion	and they lifted, a little, and our eyes, too, so all of a sudden we noticed things, like the warmth of the red sun, sinking behind us . . .
Cleopas	and that this stranger was going our way . . .
Companion	and feeding our souls as lovingly as a mother bird feeds her young, . . .
Cleopas	and that it was dusk, and we were home, and hungry!
Companion	"Stay with us," we pleaded, because we needed so much more of his mysterious balm.
Cleopas	So he did. And together we washed away the dirt and dust of that long strange day . . .
Companion	and sat down to the comfort that only an evening meal with friends can bring.
Cleopas	When our guest boldly became our host, we let him, because we were so very, very tired.
Companion	And when he took the crusty bread, blessed it, broke it, and offered it, we suddenly knew!

Cleopas	You always do, don't you,...
Companion	the look and feel and sound of real love?
Cleopas	We remembered that gaze, that touch, that fire in the chest that only he had ever stirred up before! In his love, we knew him!
Companion	And then he was gone, just like that, and we were forever changed. That grace-filled moment when he fed us turned us around, got us up from the table, and headed us back to town.
Cleopas	But this time we almost ran, and pretty soon we were shouting to a dark, sleepy Jerusalem, "He's alive! We've seen him! He's alive!"
Companion	If you have ever been on the road to Emmaus, mad, hurt, terrified, lost, feeling all alone,...
Cleopas	or if you're on that road right now, then you should remember how Jesus came to find us...
Companion	and will find you, too—no road is too far, no country too strange. He will come looking...
Cleopas	and walk beside you, going your way, keeping your pace, until your heart burns again with faith and hope, and you're ready to turn around.
Companion	You'll know him by the love with which he breaks your bread and feeds you,...
Cleopas	and touches your hand, and offers God's peace,...
Companion	and pours your coffee, and asks your help, and remembers your name...
Cleopas	and gently leads you back to the community, which isn't whole without you.
Companion	On the road to Emmaus, no matter how dark, or lonely, or far, expect to be found, and gathered,...
Cleopas	and turned round right by God's love.

THE GREAT CATCH

In the weeks following a terrible loss, the shock and pain give way to a dull, wordless ache. The best things to do are those you can do numbly, without thinking. Like skipping stones on the Sea of Tiberius as the sun sinks into the black water. Or untangling your fishing nets as you down your second cold beer. Could be your third, or fourth.

It's terrible to be alone, but even worse to be with others. Their grief on top of yours is just too much grief. Maybe you *should* get away—a little time by yourself might be just what you need.

"I'm going fishing," you say. Clearly an announcement and not an invitation, but such subtleties are lost on them these days. "Oh, yeah. Fishing. Sure, we'll go, too." And they climb behind you into the rounded wooden hull of the boat which starts to rock you like the cradle of your infancy, as though the waves knew you needed to be held.

Rowing out as far as you can, it's mostly quiet but for the slapping water, and the occasional humming, deep sigh, or wondering aloud. "Did we really see him in that room? Maybe we were hallucinating…grieving people do, you know, see things and hear things. God, how I miss him! Hard to believe it's been a whole week. Almost two. I'd give anything to have him back." Well, enough of this. A little too intimate for a boatful of guys. "Let's get to work."

"Yeah, the night's half gone. Let's get to work!" So you strip down, drop the nets, and head for shore, hoping you'll soon feel the heavy drag that means fish. And then, reaching the seaside with nothing, you turn around and do it again. And again. And again, with no luck, but who cares, what's the point? And anyway, soon it'll be dawn and you can go home to the blessed relief of a hard sleep, and mark on your calendar one more long day without him.

Heading in for the night, no one bothers to talk. There's a lone, shadowy figure standing on the sand, still a ways off, about a hundred yards, a football field's length.

"Hey! D'ja catch anything?"

Why do people always ask that? Like it's a communal event. They don't ask, when you leave the hardware store, "D'ja buy anything?" Or, when you leave the dentist, "D'ya feel better?"

But, well, folks like to know. "D'ja catch anything?"

"Nope. Not a thing."

"Try putting your nets down on the right side of the boat. Yeah. No, no, your *other* right!"

Well, fishermen will try anything. Turn their cap around. Change bait. Cast farther, closer, one more time. And do you know? It worked...and how! Now there were so many fish they could hardly keep the boat aright, much less haul in the nets.

There's something fishy about this. Mighty familiar. This feeling, this sudden turn of events, this miraculous abundance. Someone whispers, "This has Jesus written all over it."

Jesus? You throw on your clothes, backwards and inside out, and plunge into the cold sea, swimming like mad, knowing only this: You've got to get to him...got to get to him now! And when you do, he holds you close and tight while you shiver and drip.

"You must be starving," he says, "and so cold! Look at you...you're dripping wet. Come and warm yourself. Come and eat breakfast. Yeah, sure, bring some of what you just caught. It can cook while you eat what's ready."

And while he serves you the hot, salty fish and the warm crusts of bread, you wonder how it is that he always knows what you truly need and really want. And he doesn't analyze, or judge, or tell you something else would really be better for you. He just comes, and serves you, and warms you, and feeds you.

What will it take, you wonder, for you to finally know without a doubt that, somehow, he will always be there for you. Always. So tender. Right there. With just what you need.

A Jewish woman opens her door one night to loud and frantic knocking and discovers her son, badly beaten, bloody, and terrified. "Mother, they're after me! They're trying to kill me! You have to hide me. Help me, please!" She drags her son through the door, bolts it shut and says, "First eat. Then we'll talk!"

So he says to us: First eat. Then we'll talk. Yeah, yeah, I know all the reasons you don't deserve it, don't deserve me. First eat. Then we'll talk.

May we then, first, let him feed us, with just what we need, from the fullness of his heart, with the tenderness of his hands, and the warmth of his presence.

A Story of Freedom

A Dramatic Reading for Three People

Paul should be stage-center, with the Slave Girl and the Jailer on either side of him.

Paul	Freedom, you know, is a funny thing. Because it's possible to be locked away in the innermost cell of a prison, and yet still, somehow, your heart can sing, like a stream running free!
Jailer	And it's possible to believe you're free, but you might just as well be bound hand and foot, because you can't seem to choose for yourself what's really right and good.
Paul	Like the slave girl who followed Silas and me through the streets of Philippi. Talk about bondage! Even her thoughts weren't her own!
Slave Girl	But my owners were even less free than I, they were so bound by greed, which steals your heart and makes you treat others as things to be used. Like how they used me to tell fortunes, making a fortune of their own!
Paul	But something inside her remained untouched, utterly free, which was how she knew the truth of our words, and loudly said so, to all the folks in town.
Slave Girl	Listen, people! These men bring us a way of salvation! Listen and hear, and be free!
Jailer	Freedom can be costly. Just ask her owners, who first lost themselves by exploiting that girl, and then, when Paul and Silas healed her, lost their meal ticket! Which made them so mad they had the apostles thrown in my jail.
Paul	But not before we were stripped and beaten and placed in stocks in the innermost cell of the prison. The jailer was kind and good, but we had to wonder, how free was he, spending all his days in the company of the chained?

Jailer	I was a middle management type caught between those above me, who made me so afraid, and those below me, who made me so sad. My heart was all torn, and weary, and confused.
Paul	Well, we cheered ourselves by praying and singing hymns. Some of the other prisoners sang with us but the jailer didn't know the words.
Jailer	I don't know how I slept through the earthquake, but I did, and when I saw how the doors were all opened, the chains all unlocked, I drew my sword and was ready to take my own life. I was as good as dead, anyway, now, having failed at my sad job.
Slave Girl	But no one had left! And, even without the lights, for which he called right away, the jailer could see hope shining everywhere around all of the prisoners, as they shared the good news of Jesus, and he went and joined them all, on his knees.
Jailer	In a flash, my heart grew brave and saw something it wanted, more than anything, ever. "Sirs, what must I do to be saved?" I asked, thinking, of course, it would be something quite hard, but knowing I'd do it, whatever it was.
Paul	Just believe, we said. Only believe. Just believe in Jesus, and you will be saved, you and your household.
Jailer	So I did. I believed. And then I took them home, and gently washed their bruises and wounds, and then they washed me, and my family too, with the waters of life, and we all were saved.
Slave Girl	Freedom, indeed, is a strange and wonderful thing, coming, as it does, from someone, or something, outside all our locked doors, . . .
Paul	or from someplace deep inside, where no one can touch it, or steal it away.
Slave Girl	God wants us free!
Paul	And when we are all bound up in the deepest innermost cells of our darkest prisons, . . .
Slave Girl	convinced we are hopeless, abandoned, and lost, . . .
Jailer	God will come find us, bringing light to our darkness, and whispering love to our hungry hearts.
Paul	God will find us in our chains and break their hold, and bring us again to the light of day.

Slave Girl	And when we are wounded and scarred from bondages past, God will tenderly wash and restore us, and give us new life, new every morning.
Jailer	Because God wants us free. No matter who you are or what you've sold your heart to, be it money or slavery or fear,
Slave Girl	God wants to buy you back. God wants you free, and will move the earth and the seas to make it so.
Paul	Freedom is a funny thing, because the freedom that is truly free is the love that girds and binds us, leading us home to ourselves and then out again to where we can serve, any and all who need us.

PENTECOST AND PILGRIMAGE

A Story for the Feast of Pentecost

Do you know what a pilgrim is? A pilgrim is someone who is on the move! All God's people are pilgrims, always on the move.

Our father, Abraham, and our mother, Sarah, were on the move, traveling wherever they could find grazing for their animals. One day God said to them, "Abraham! Sarah! Take your family, your belongings, and animals, and leave this dry land. Go yonder, to a better place, a lush, green place, flowing with milk and honey, and dripping with fruit. I will give you that place for your home, forever! For your children, and your children's children, and your children's children's children!"

So they did. Abraham and Sarah moved to that lush place and started to put down roots. They planted things. They planted themselves! But there came a drought that choked the rich, wet earth, and a famine set in, starving people and animals alike.

And so they were on the move again, going down to Egypt-land, where they could eat, and where their family grew for four hundred years into a huge nation of thousands of people, and they didn't have to be on the move. But that was the problem. They *couldn't* move, because in Egypt they became slaves. In their slavery the people cried out and God heard their cries and remembered the ancient promise. It was time for Abraham and Sarah and their huge family to be on the move again.

In the dark of a warm, spring night, they packed all their things, and ate their last meal in Egypt. It was a Passover meal, made so fast that they didn't have time to let their bread rise! They ate unleavened flatbread, and, with their kneading bowls in their arms and their children on their shoulders, they fled from their bondage in Egypt. God led them through the Red Sea waters, which stood up high on either side to let them pass, and crashed back down again on the Egyptians who were chasing them.

Across the sea, in the desert, God cared for the people like a mother cares for her children, sending manna and quail for food, and, for drink, making water to flow from rocks. After several months God said to Moses, "I want to speak to the people. Help them get ready."

For three days the people got ready to listen to God. Never before had they heard the Voice of God, and they were afraid. How would it sound? What would God say?

When the people gathered at the foot of Mount Sinai, there was thunder, and lightning, and a trumpet blast, and the whole mountain shook, and God came down like fire on the mountain and wrapped it in smoke. They heard no voice, so Moses disappeared into the smoke, climbing up the mountain alone to talk with God. When he came down, his face shone like the sun, and he held in his hands the two tablets of Torah, God's laws for a life of health and peace.

That day, at the foot of Mount Sinai, God married the Jewish people. The mountain was like a wedding canopy, a huge, lovely *chuppah*. God thought the people were as beautiful as the moon and as radiant as the sun, and God loved them fiercely. God made vows, saying, "If you will be my people, I will be your God," and the people, Israel, the bride of God, said, "Yes, I will. I do, Yes."

For forty years in that desert wilderness the people were wandering, moving, but they weren't getting anywhere! And then came the time to head toward home. They crossed the Jordan River into Canaan and built homes, and planted fields, and settled in for many, many years. Some were good years, and peaceful, and others were filled with wars and sadness, but at least they were home.

But even at home the people were still pilgrims. Because every year at the holy days, the Jewish people all over Canaan-land would be on the move, traveling to Jerusalem, and flooding its streets with feasting, and long processions of dancing and song, all the way up to the Temple.

At Succoth, when the fall harvest was in, they would make a pilgrimage to the holy city bringing their vegetables and grain to the altar.

And at Pesach, in the spring, they would go to Jerusalem and eat a Seder meal, with the Passover lamb, and the bitter herbs, and the unleavened flatbread, telling the children of their narrow escape from Egypt in the dark of night. And then the people would go home, and begin to count the days:

One, two, three, four, five, six, seven days, one week. Eight, nine, ten, eleven, twelve, thirteen, fourteen days, two weeks. And so on, until they had counted forty-nine days, seven whole weeks.

And then back to Jerusalem they would go, to celebrate the feast of weeks, Shavuot, Pentecost, a celebration of spring and the first harvest of wheat.

Every year, year after year, the people would be pilgrims, traveling to the holy city Jerusalem for Succoth and Passover and Pentecost, Succoth, Passover, Pentecost. On the move, dancing, singing, and feasting, Succoth, Passover, Pentecost.

One of those years, at Pentecost, among the pilgrims were Peter, James, John, Mary, Salome, Andrew, Simon, Joanna, and all of the friends and followers of Jesus, about a hundred and twenty in all. They were waiting in Jerusalem for something Jesus had promised to send them, they didn't know what. They were remembering that great wedding day at Sinai when God had come down like fire and spoken to Moses who had brought the Torah down to the Jewish people, blessing them forever with its honey-like sweetness. They were sitting, talking, remembering, and waiting.

Suddenly, God came down again like fire! Only this time, the fire wasn't far away, on the distant top of a mountain. Now it was close, resting on the head of each person. And God spoke again! Not to just one man, like at Sinai, but to every person there! And with great joy and noise they told of God's love, so loudly that all Jerusalem gathered outside to hear, and it was in many languages (just like today), so that there was not one person in the city who could not hear and understand the love of God. When they left that room they went on the longest, greatest, widest pilgrimage ever, spreading over the whole world to tell of Jesus.

I think there are many ways to be a pilgrim.
> We can travel to faraway lands to keep holy days and pray in sacred places.
> We can travel near or far to carry God's love in our words and deeds.
> We can move from here to there, following where God leads, to learn or to work.
> We can go to our neighbors, and offer help, and good news.

But maybe a pilgrim can be someone who sits still, stays put, sending down roots, making a home, but moving on the inside, silently, secretly, toward more love, or faith, or forgiveness, or courage.

Pentecost says God's love never stops moving, even if it's only a tiny step forward or inward, and that the restless love of God lives, not on some distant mountain, not long ago and far away, but here, now, in the warm, fleshy hearts of us all.

Maya Angelou wrote, "All God's children need traveling shoes; we're moving on." We are pilgrims, whose souls are shod in traveling shoes so the Spirit can always be moving us on, moving us on.

Amen.

Spirit God

Susan K. Bock

Copyright © 2008 Susan K. Bock

The Season after Pentecost

Ordinary Time

God of seasons and Sabbath,
God of our days and our hearts:
You bless us with greening time,
that we might be renewed.

Teach us to live slowly,
and taste the goodness of your love.

Show us how every moment
is alive with you,
far from ordinary,
trembling with hope,
shining with glory.

Through Christ,
who found you in corners of quiet,
and in whose arms we find rest.

Amen.

THE PRAYERS OF THE PEOPLE FOR THE CHILDREN OF GOD

Let us pray for the church and the world, and for all God's children.

For all the children in the world, for the eternal and enduring Child in all people, and for the childlikeness which grasps your truth and to which we are called,
   We thank you, Lord.

For each child that you have given into our care in this *parish, school*; for their gifts, talents, and love, and for the privilege of sharing with them the journey of faith,
   We thank you, Lord.

For all of those who share their time with children to guide and learn from them; for parents, teachers, and volunteers; for *N, N,* and *N,* whose work in this place graces us all,
   We thank you, Lord.

For the gift of Holy Baptism, through which we are all born anew and by which you give us, young and old, to be sisters and brothers to each other, [and especially for *N, N,* and *N,* as *they* prepare to be baptized on *All Saints' Day, Easter Eve, next Sunday,*]
   We thank you, Lord.

We lift up to you the needs of all children everywhere. For those who are hungry and afflicted by war,
   Hear us, Lord.

For those who are sick with AIDS, cancer, and other diseases,
   Hear us, Lord.

For runaways and for refugees; for victims of abuse and neglect,
   Hear us, Lord.

For those who are prevented in any way from realizing the growth, abundance, and freedom that is their birthright,
   Hear us, Lord.

To all organizations that work for the well-being of children, [especially *(specific and local agencies may be named),*]
   Grant wisdom, grace, and strength, O God.

To all those in authority who make decisions for the world's children; to presidents, rulers, and legislators,
    Grant wisdom, grace, and strength, O God.

To each of us charged with stewardship of our environment, that the children of the future might have fresh air and clean water,
    Grant wisdom, grace, and strength, O God.

Gracious and ever-living God, whose Child Jesus shows us how full is your heart with love toward us all: Grant that we, like him, may take up your call to live and walk in that love, and to rest and play and work with the freedom of children, and always on their behalf; through Christ our Lord.
    Amen.

Jairus' Daughter and the Bleeding Woman

Having crossed the sea for rest, but finding none, Jesus had sailed back home. Before he even stepped off the boat, they had gathered again. By the hundreds.

While he was teaching them, Jairus, a ruler of the synagogue, pushed his way through the crowd and threw himself at his feet. "My little girl is dying! Come, please. Please. Please come and lay your hands upon her, that she might live."

And immediately he went, the crowd close in tow, followed at some distance by a woman who had suffered a flow of menstrual blood for twelve years! Making her unclean. And anyone she touched, unclean. And anyone who touched what she touched, unclean. All that time.

Suddenly, she was seized by the strangest idea. Irresistible, really, because she found herself pushing through the wall of people and reaching for him. "You can't touch him!" she told herself.

"Just touch him!" she answered herself back.

The crowd pressed and squeezed and carried her along, but he stayed just beyond her reach. And so, with her last little bit of strength and hope, she thrust her arm forward and touched him!

Well, just his robe. But she had reached him! And she felt in her body that she was healed, and let herself fall back and away.

Immediately he spun on his heels and shouted, "Who touched me?"

"Teacher," said his friends, "who *didn't* touch you?! We can barely walk! We can hardly breathe, for all these people."

"No, someone touched me." And he began to search the sea of faces for the one whose faith could pull such power from him.

And she came and fell at his feet and told him everything. So he knelt and lifted her chin, and with a word, "Daughter," he restored her to the community. "Daughter, your faith has made you well."

Jairus looked on, amazed. Just then, some people came from his home. "It's too late," they said. "Don't trouble him anymore." (And for God's sake, man, don't bring him to your house! Have you forgotten who you are?)

Jairus looked at Jesus, and the woman, and they looked back. And for a brief, magic moment, there were just those three, holding each others' gaze, while the crowd faded away, like in a movie.

"Don't be afraid," said Jesus. "Only believe."

So he did. He believed. And they continued on their way, arm in arm: a man who ruled the synagogue, a woman of the lowliest estate, and this strange, grace-filled healer who restored the child too that day, taking her by the hand and calling her up from her bed of death.

"Get up!" he said. And she did. She got up and Jesus gave her back to her parents, who covered her with tears and held her like they'd never, ever let go.

Elijah Passes His Mantle

A Dramatic Reading for Three Readers

Reader   It was the very end of Elijah's life. Time to say good-bye. Time to let go. He and Elisha were leaving Gilgal, and walking toward Bethel. Maybe he didn't know *how* to do it, how to say good-bye: to his work, his amazing, terrible, wonderful work; to this sweet world; to Elisha, the companion of his heart. So he said to Elisha,

Elijah   You stay here. God has told me to go to Bethel, but it's a long way, and, really, I'll be fine.

Reader   But Elisha said,

Elisha   As the Lord lives, and as you yourself live, I will not leave you!

Reader   So together they walked all the way to Bethel. And maybe Elijah was afraid he would cry, because he said,

Elijah   You stay here. God has told me to go all the way to Jericho. But it's a long, long way, and you're young, and there's no point in both of us wearing out our sandals, blistering our feet.

Reader   But Elisha said,

Elisha   As the Lord lives, and as you yourself live, I will not leave you!

Reader   So together they walked all the way to Jericho. Sometimes they talked, but mostly each was alone in his thoughts, each one trying to imagine his life without the other. And maybe Elijah was trying to spare Elisha the pain of his leaving, or the weight of his calling, because he said,

Elijah   You stay here. The Lord has sent me yonder to the Jordan, but there's nothing there for you to do. I mean, have you ever been to the Jordan? Small, muddy…no, no, you stay here.

Reader   But Elisha said,

Elisha	As the Lord lives and as you yourself live,...
Reader	"Oi! What a will!" thought Elijah.
Elisha	I will not leave you!
Reader	So together they went on to the Jordan and, as they stood at its edge, fifty meddlesome prophets looked on. And Elijah took his mantle, rolled it up, and struck the water. And the water parted and stood up on either side, just like the Red Sea waters, and let them pass through, together, on dry ground. On the far side of the river, Elijah said to Elisha,
Elijah	Tell me what I may do for you.
Reader	By which he might have meant, "What do I have to do to get you to let me go?" And Elisha said,
Elisha	I want a spirit like yours, courageous and true, only more so, double the measure of yours!
Reader	And Elijah thought, "How can I ask this for someone I love so much? It was hard enough being me, and he wants to be more than that?" But in Elisha's eyes, Elijah could see all the way to the young man's heart, and he knew there was no use, that he was eager, hungry, for God. So he said,
Elijah	As I am leaving, watch me go, and if you can see me, what you ask will be given.
Reader	When the fiery chariots came, and whirled Elijah up to the heavens, Elisha watched, though he was afraid, though his eyes burned and clouded with tears, still he watched, till Elijah was just a speck in the sky, and then he was gone, and Elisha fell to the ground and wept aloud in grief. When he looked up, there was Elijah's mantle, which he scooped up and held to his heart and his face, breathing in the familiar scent of his master, and then he picked himself up and turned toward home.
	At the Jordan, Elisha struck the waters, which now parted for him, and then he knew, and all the prophets watching knew, that the spirit of Elijah had come to rest on him.

Elijah Passes His Mantle

A Skit for Two People, with a Narrator

*Elijah and Elisha mostly address the listeners (all the lines in **bold print**).
Otherwise, they speak to each other. This is easiest if the actors begin at the
entrance of the nave, and continue all the way up to the sanctuary. When they
begin, Elijah is wearing a "mantle" or stole. The narrator should be off to the
side, at a lectern or pulpit.*

Narrator	Now when the Lord was about to take Elijah up to heaven, Elijah and Elisha were on their way from Gilgal. Elijah said to Elisha,
Elijah	You stay here. I am going on to Bethel, where the Lord has sent me.
Elisha	**This is one of those God moments, I can smell it! I can feel Elijah leaving, going somewhere I won't be able to see him or hear him.**
Elijah	**It's not easy being a prophet, speaking for God!**
Elisha	**But *I* can't speak for God!**
Elijah	**I'm so tired.**
Elisha	**Not without him! I'm so scared.**
Elijah	**Only my zeal for the Lord has kept me going, all this time. And Elisha, of course. What a wonder of courage and love!**
Elisha	**I really love that old guy.**
Elijah	**Reminds me of ... well, he reminds me of me, how I was a few years ago. . . . Okay, a *lot* of years ago!**
Elisha	As the Lord lives, and as you yourself live, I will not leave you!
Elijah	**Oi! What a will!**

LITURGY FOR THE WHOLE CHURCH / SUSAN K. BOCK

Elisha	How can I ever let him go?
Elijah	How can I leave him? There is still so much to do…
Elisha	still so much to say.
Elijah	Well then, come, if you must, but only as far as the Jordan.
Elijah and Elisha	I remember the first time I saw him….
Elisha	I was plowing our fields, just minding my business.
Elijah	He was driving oxen, twelve teams of the great, stubborn beasts, and I thought, "Hmm. Good training for guiding the people of God!"
Elisha	When he threw his mantle over my head, well, he caught my heart, too, and all my hopes and dreams. I just *had* to go with him!
Narrator	When they came to the Jordan, Elijah took his mantle and rolled it up and struck the water. The water was parted to one side and to the other, and the two of them crossed over on dry ground.
Elisha	It's a God moment, for sure! When the waters stand up, letting you pass between them, there's no saying "no." You can't go back. You can only go *through*.
Elijah	Tell me what I may do for you, before I am taken away from you.
Elisha	*(kneeling before him)* Please let me have a double share of your spirit.
Elijah	For twice the work? How can I wish that for you?!
Elisha	For twice the wisdom, and twice the courage. For twice the love to *do* the work.
Elijah	*(kneeling, too, to meet Elisha's eyes)* If you see me as I am being taken away from you, then know that it will be so. You will be given all that I have, and more.

As the Narrator continues, Elijah should remove his mantle, place it on the ground, and move ahead of Elisha, while Elisha stops and looks up.

Narrator	Suddenly, a chariot and horses of fire came between them, and Elijah was swept up into heaven by a whirlwind. Elisha watched as far as he could, and kept crying out,
Elisha	Father, Father! The chariots of Israel and its horsemen!
Narrator	But when he could no longer see him, he tore his clothes in grief. Then he picked up the mantle of Elijah that had fallen on the ground and stood again at the bank of the Jordan River.

Elisha can pick up the mantle and hold it heavenward.

Narrator	He took the mantle of Elijah and struck the water, saying,
Elisha	*(loudly and with passion)* Where is the Lord, the God of Elijah?
Narrator	And the water was parted to one side and to the other, and Elisha went over on dry ground.

Elisha dons the mantle and walks on.

Narrator	And when all the other prophets saw Elisha returning, they said, "The spirit of Elijah rests on Elisha!"

COME AND REST. REALLY.

Reader Come to me, all who labor and are heavy laden, and I will refresh you. Take my yoke upon you. Learn from me. For I am gentle and humble of heart. You shall find rest for your soul. For my yoke is easy. My burden is light.

As the words are being read, Heavy-Laden Guy (HLG) enters, struggling, laboring under his burden, a huge sack of "problems"—packages wrapped up in various ways. Jesus enters from the other side, and is listening in, but HLG doesn't see him.

HLG *(to listeners)* Yeah, yeah, I've heard it all before. But, could it really be true? I mean, it sounds too good. The very words make you want to sigh with relief: come; rest; gentle; humble; easy; light. They sound like a song. But, could they be true? That's what I'd ask him if we ever met up.

Jesus Hey, what have you got there?

HLG *(surprised and embarrassed)* Oh! Lots of important things I can't do without.

Jesus Like what?

HLG Well, you know, I've got worry. *(HLG unloads a big package.)* That's the biggest thing. There's so much to worry about: money, and my health, and my kids and other people's kids, and my parents and other people's parents, the church, global warming, terrorism, the stock market, Social Security…and whether anyone really likes me!

Jesus That *is* a lot of stuff! I wonder what your life would be like if you gave up all that worry.

HLG ponders this.

Jesus What else have you got in that big bag of important stuff?

HLG Well, ah, there's guilt. And regrets: If only I'd done this, what if I'd done that; why did I, or why didn't I, etc.…

Jesus	You know, you could spend so much of *today* regretting *yesterday* that by *tomorrow* you'd be regretting *today*!
HLG	Wow! *(to listeners)* And while I'm pondering that, he starts snooping around in my bundle!
Jesus	What else is in there?
HLG	Well *(rummaging through)*, there's shame. And inferiority. There's resentment, and judgments, and anger. There's prejudice, and grief, and boredom, and, oops... *(closing it quickly)*. Uh...that's all!
Jesus	C'mon. What else is in there?
HLG	Okay. There's just this last little thing. It's fear.
Jesus	*(very gently)* What are you afraid of?
HLG	Everything. But my shadow. No, I'm afraid of that, too. I'm afraid to try things. Afraid not to. Afraid to offer my talents, gifts, and ideas. Afraid of growing up. Getting old. Moving on. Staying put. Afraid of dying. Afraid of living. Afraid of loving.
Jesus	Good heavens, that must be heavy!
HLG	You know it! *(And then, to listeners)* So now I'm thinking, maybe he'll help me. You know, with a little help, maybe I *could* manage it all!
Jesus	You should put it all back in the bag.
HLG	*(still to listeners)* Okay, I think, maybe he's just going to send me off with a blessing and a prayer, which is very kind, very Christ-like, and all. But then he proposes a trade!
Jesus	I'll take that for you.
HLG	All of it?
Jesus	Yeah. I'll take it all. I'll carry it for you.
HLG	*(very suspiciously, and hiding his bundle protectively behind him)* Why?
Jesus	Because you're tired. You need rest. And because that's what I do. I take the burdens and I sort them out.
HLG	What do you do with them all?

Jesus	Well, some of them—the old, tired stuff, and the useless lies—I just banish. And some don't even belong to you, so I give them back to the person who really owns them. And some of them, like grief, I put back, but just a little at a time, so you can walk it out, and travel with it where you need to go, and put it down yourself when it's time.
HLG	Hmmmmm. You would really take this whole bag of burdens?
Jesus	I would.
HLG	But that's kind of scary. Because, you know, my fear is still mine, after all. And without my big heavy sack, what would I do? What would I do with my newly straightened back, and my new perspective, and my new, lighter step? What would I do with my new freedom? What would I do with my hands?
Jesus	What a very good thing to spend some time wondering about!
HLG	*(to listeners)* So, I pack up my bag, and hand it over to him. And he takes it. The whole thing!
Jesus	Now. Here's the trade.
HLG	*(to listeners)* Oh, *man*! I had forgotten it was a trade.
Jesus	In return for the bundle, I want to give you my yoke.
HLG	A *yoke*!? A yoke is, well, it's one of those big wooden brackets that a farmer uses to team up his oxen. So they can walk together and work together. Oh, brother. A yoke. I don't know…. *(He walks away to think, and speaks to the listeners.)* So I weigh it all out: his yoke, my bundle. My bundle, his yoke. I choose the yoke. And then I hunker down and get ready to be harnessed up and suddenly remember to ask: WAIT! Who am I going to be yoked with? I mean, that could make all the difference, you know?
Jesus	Oh, well, here's the thing. It's me.
HLG	I'll be yoked to you?
Jesus	So you can walk with me. And when you're tired, I can kneel at your feet, and wash them, and refresh you, and you'll be able to keep on your journey.
HLG	All right. Your yoke, with you beside me.
Jesus	Yep.

HLG	And all I gotta do is give you my bundle?
Jesus	Yep.
HLG	Doesn't seem fair.
Jesus	Nope. I don't really do "fair." My specialty is grace.
HLG	Okay. Let's have it. *(to listeners)* I close my eyes. I wait for the yoke. His yoke. To lock me up, lock me in, lock me down. Whatever. And then he slips his warm arm around my waist, so gentle and loving, and off we go.

They can leave down the aisle, arm in arm, as HLG concludes:

HLG	My burdens for his yoke. My bundle for his companionship. Rest, refreshment, and grace. *(A pause and big sigh.)* I definitely got the sweet end of the deal!

A Story of King David

The thing about David was that he devoured life, swallowed it whole, squeezed every drop out of every minute, feeling it all, from the heights of joy to the depths of despair, weeping and wailing and rending his clothes when his heart got broke, leaping and dancing and laughing, nearly naked, in his joy for God. He loved everything and everyone as deeply and widely as love can go, and loved as many women as his hands and eyes could reach!

The women loved him back. Everyone did. Well, everyone but Saul. Saul hated him. It was pure envy because there was nothing, it seemed, that David couldn't do. He was a man of valor, with a godly presence and prudent speech. He was a brave and brilliant warrior, a gifted musician and poet. Plus, he could dance. Wildly!

His heart was full to bursting with every good thing, like justice and pity. He was wide open to all that life had to offer and you always knew how he felt, and what he was thinking. None of that strong, silent stuff. And God's favor toward him was as bright and clear and sure as the sunrise.

But one day David did a terrible thing and his whole world collapsed. He stole another man's wife for himself, the lovely Bathsheba, breaking her marriage to Uriah, one of David's best soldiers. Then he wove around the whole mess a killing web of lies that ended in Uriah's death and Bathsheba's moving into the palace and, when Nathan the prophet came to call, it wasn't with a covered dish!

"What should happen," asked Nathan, "to the man who steals a beloved lamb from the bosom of someone lesser than he?"

"Well, that man should die, of course!" said David.

"But you are the man," said Nathan. "You. You are the man."

Oh, those dreadful moments of sudden knowing, of seeing yourself and the shameful thing you have done in the harsh light of truth. How do you keep breathing? How will you ever go on living with such crushing shame and regret?

When Nathan predicted the death of Bathsheba's baby, David grieved like David did everything: with heart and body and soul. He grieved over the loss of the child. He grieved over the loss of himself.

He wished himself dead. He tried to die. He lay on the ground, weeping, keening, for seven whole days. He refused to eat or drink. He would not be comforted. He pleaded with God, then cursed God, then pleaded again. Maybe God would see his grief and rescue him from this terror. Maybe this was a horrible dream and he would soon awaken to life as it once was. Maybe he could just lie there and not move, barely breathing, his eyes closed, and the darkness he'd made for himself would just fade away and take him with it.

But the child died, and David kept on living. And so he rose, and washed, and changed his clothes, and ate and drank, and took himself into the house of God to worship the One who had never left him, even through all the desolation and terror and sin, though he didn't know it until that moment at prayer.

And, though he carried his grief forever like a man with a limp, and though it forever changed him, David returned to the land of the living, and served the Lord and the people of God all his days, with a truer, more tender, more open heart, and most of the joy, and a lot more wisdom and care than ever before.

THE GOOD SAMARITAN

Though he was a Jew, and upright in every way—keeping the Sabbath, paying his temple tax, fasting on holy days—and though he was ritually pure as well, and though, because of these things, he expected God's favor and protection, still, in spite of all the good he did and his solid trust in God, one day he found himself a heap of bloody flesh, left for dead on the road down to Jericho. Except for the flowing of his tears, he was utterly unable to move.

Stripped of his clothes, his money, and worse, his dignity, innocence, and beliefs, he thought, with a jolt, "Evidently, things are not like I've always thought they were."

Suddenly, with his ear pressed to the ground, he heard the soft thud of footsteps coming near, then a long pause, then footsteps again, retreating. He couldn't believe what he saw! It was a priest, who surely knew the law, how it says: "Refuse no one the good that is in your power to do. You must help your neighbor, that is, whoever happens to be near you."

The priest, of course, had not seen a neighbor, or even a fellow Jew. He saw a corpse, and a source of impurity. And a priest, too important and good, couldn't get sidetracked from his holy work and life, so he scurried by while the broken man lay on in the hot sun, his life slowly seeping away, and despair settling in, like a rigor mortis of the heart.

Then again there were footsteps. And hope. A pause. And then, footsteps, fading again.

It was a Levite this time, an assistant to the priests. He crossed the road. He came near enough to touch him. He reached out, and then, fearing it was a trap, pulled back his hand, wrapped his garment close, and shuffled on, nervously glancing back.

Now something new swept over the injured man. It was shame. What ought to have brought those good men near had sent them running in terror and disgust. Why do we do that to each other, he wondered, adding sorrow to sorrow? Then he heard, a third time, footsteps.

Gathering his last shreds of dignity and will, he closed his eyes to another round of cruel indifference. At least he didn't have to watch it. Again, there was the dreadful pause on which the whole world might turn, and the footsteps drawing closer, faster.

He braced himself for a kick, a brutal search. But, instead, there was a cool and gentle touch, and a low and tender voice, caught with sadness. When he was lifted onto the grass, he saw the face of a Samaritan, one of those hated half-Jews. A good Jew would rather add days to a journey than to travel through Samaritan territory. So his heart cringed but his flesh sighed with relief. And in the loving, pitying hands of this Samaritan, his rage and shame began to melt away.

The Samaritan poured wine and oil into the bloody wounds, and wrapped them with strips torn from his own clothing. He tenderly lifted the man onto his own donkey, and guided it slowly to an inn, where he tended to the wounded one all through the night. And then he left provision for his convalescence, and promised to return to be sure he was well.

The Jew learned more from the Samaritan that day than all his years of studying Torah.

"The word is very near you," Moses had said, "in your mouth and on your heart, so that you may do it."

All his life, this Samaritan, this foreigner, had experienced at the hands of good folks like himself the humiliation and shame that he had endured in this one hateful afternoon. The word was written in the Samaritan's heart, to be sure, and left no room for bitterness, or fear, or lines drawn in the sand.

He learned that the heart of the God's law is love. Its intention is love. And that laws and creeds and codes and principles are meant to bind us all together in deeper love and community, and, when they cease to do so, they should be set aside. And that the shame and guilt and blame we attach to suffering, ours and others, serves only to deepen pain.

And he was reminded of some things he'd always known, but might have come close to forgetting, like love is in the doing of what we say we believe. And purity is a matter of the heart. And a neighbor is anyone at all who needs us.

Martha and Mary

A Dramatic Reading for Two Women

Each reader addresses the listeners. Mary could be costumed with a shawl or veil, and Martha with an apron.

Martha	The "better portion"? Better for whom, I wondered. Maybe for those hungry men who stood around awaiting the daily miracle of a meal, but certainly not for me. And if I didn't fix it, who would?
Mary	It's always been this way, you know? For Martha and me, for our mother, and hers before her. We're told to love the Torah and to live by its every word, but then we're forbidden to study it! Only men may do so. The same men who argue and chew it and suck it dry till it has to taste like a mouthful of sand!
Martha	They would talk and talk, debating Torah and the meaning of life. And then the moment their stomachs growled, here they'd come, never wondering how that hot, savory food suddenly appeared, just in time. And they'd eat and eat, till they had their fill and off they'd go again, in search of great truths.
Mary	I wanted, myself, to taste its sweetness, dripping like honey. To wrap my own heart around it, and eat of its goodness until I was full. I used to hope that someday things would change, that a woman's worth could be measured by her love for God. I longed to just sit, and listen, and think. To just *be*. But there was always so much to be done!
Martha	Food is love, you know, and I needed a way to show my love. I'm a really good cook, a culinary magician! I can turn a mess of lentils into a warm, rich stew that strengthens the mind, and warms the heart...all by way of the belly! But sometimes, when the men had all gone, and I was left with a kitchen full of dishes, and a feeling as empty as their stomachs were full, I would wonder, "Is this all there is for me?" Well, it's always been this way...for me, for my mother, for hers before her. If I didn't do it, who would?

Mary	When Jesus first started coming around, I just shadowed Martha, cooking, serving, waiting. She is so competent! Everything she touches is lovely and tasty and fine! Really, I just wanted to be near the men, listening and learning. His words were so fresh and new, and, secretly, I hung on each one...
Martha	while the bread burned and the soup boiled over!
Mary	Then she'd get angry, and heave a weary sigh. And I would feel sorry and sad.
Martha	"In my next life," she'd grumble, "I'm going to be a man!"
Mary	One day, he looked up and saw all this, though men rarely bother to look as far as the kitchen. But he did.
Martha	And he came to where we were, and took the things from our hands, and gently led us to where the others waited,...
Mary	still scratching their heads over the last amazing thing he had said!
Martha	I sat as still as I could that day, at his feet. But my mind was cluttered and frantic with all there was still to do. There was no mistaking his words, or how he looked right at me when he said them: "Blessed is everyone who hears God's word and does it."
Mary	You could tell they were thinking, "What's going on here, and who's in the kitchen?" But he just smiled, seating us closer to him. "Blessed are *all* of those," he said, "who hear the word of God and keep it."
Martha	My hands felt empty and restless and I was fretful as can be. "Who's going to make supper?" I thought. "If I don't do it...if I don't do it...." And suddenly I knew the real questions under all that worry: If I don't do it, if I don't do it *all*, with *ease* and *flair*, then who am I? Why am I here? Who will need me? And if no one needs me, will anyone love me?
	And I was just too afraid to sit and wait for those answers to speak from my heart. So I leapt up and got as busy as I could, leaving no room for thought, just that familiar, anxious, exhausted smolder. And there was Mary, on the edge of some social frontier! How dare she sit like that, all quiet and still, when I was so overwhelmed? "If you want supper," I called, as sweetly as I could, "you'd better send Mary in here to help."
Mary	"Martha," he said...
Martha	I did love the sound of my name when he spoke it.

Mary	"Martha, no one loves a good meal better than I, and it all has to be done. But our first duty, yours and mine, is to feed the flame of love in our hearts. Our food, yours and mine, is every word that comes from the mouth of our God, who feeds our hungry souls like a mother bird tending her young."
Martha	"So come," he said. "Come and join your sister, and your brothers, and me, while we try to make a little space for God in the midst of the cares of the day. For, if we don't do it, who will?"
Mary	So she did. She came and sat down, at his feet.
Martha	And I couldn't get him close enough.
Mary	And neither could I. And now that he's gone, I meet him still in the quiet of my heart, and in the sweet company of our gatherings, and in the stories we tell to remember, and even in the words of Torah, which I study now for myself!
Martha	And I have learned to let go. To put it all down.

Here the reader may drop her apron on the chancel steps, and the two women may sit together on the chancel steps.

Martha	To let things wait. To just sit, and breathe, and *be*. Can you imagine?

A slight, reflective pause.

Martha	And it is better. And the better part of me.
Mary	The best thing. The only thing, really, that's needed.
Martha	And, somehow, it all gets done...
Mary	and the lentils taste better than ever...
Martha	and no one is angry or empty or sad, because somehow it's like he feeds us himself, with his own sweet presence and love.
Mary	And what could be better than that?

LOAVES AND FISHES

When you're bone-weary, dog-tired, utterly spent, empty-handed and empty-hearted, all you want is the perfect peace of some time alone, so your soul can water its own garden, and you can whisper your deepest fear and dearest longings to the One who dwells inside you, and waits there, always, for you to come home to yourself.

That's what he needed—time alone, and no one's hungry eyes asking for help or hope. Time to wonder, and brood, and watch clouds, and to remember the God of his heart.

So he took his best friends (because time with a true friend is almost as good as time alone with just you, and because they needed rest, too) and stole away to a secret place where no one would ever be able to find them, ever.

But they did. By the thousands. And when he saw them, his heart just sank. Only, when it hit bottom, where he was sure there was nothing left to give, it found there this well of compassion, rising like a spring, and soon it was flowing out like a mighty flood through his every pore, and he was teaching and healing for all he was worth, and it felt just right.

So he didn't notice the sun sinking below the horizon, or the growing chill on the air. But his disciples did.

"What happened to our vacation?" they grumbled, checking their watches, rolling their eyes, tapping their feet. "Lord, it's late and you've done enough. Send them away to find their supper."

"Supper?" he said. And just then his stomach growled really loudly, for he'd quite forgotten all day about food. "Supper sounds great! Let's just eat here—there's still so much to do. Could you guys arrange it while I just, uh, one, a few more.... "

"Lord, that's impossible!" they say.

"Impossible?"

"Yeah. Impossible. All we've got are these two dried fish and five little barley loaves."

Now, he loves that word, impossible, because every time it's uttered in God's hearing, things happen. Miraculous things. Impossible things.

They bring him the fish and the bread. "This is all we have!" they say.

"Oh," he says, taking them in his hands and holding them as precious things, priceless things. "You have all this? Make the people sit down. Have them sit in the cool, green grass, and rest, and wait. Yeah, sit them down."

(Can you hear all that's in those words? Sit yourself down. Rest for awhile. Feel the earth beneath you, cradling you like a mother. And trust her. For just a few moments, give up the frantic, hungry, fearful drive to be your own provider, your own god. Breathe. Open your hands. Open your heart. Breathe again. Let yourself be cared for. Sit your *heart* down.)

So they did. All of them. Even the disciples. And Jesus looked to heaven and blessed God for those gifts—meager, lovely, perfect things. And then he broke them into pieces and shared them around till all had had their fill and were satisfied.

(Does your heart hear the sound of that word, "satisfied"? Close your eyes and imagine yourself satisfied. No grasping for a future. No regretting of the past. Only a deep knowing that here, now, what you have and who you are is enough. Because God is with you, here and now, and God satisfies like nothing else ever can.)

Satisfied is what they felt, that cool green evening. All of them, even the disciples, and Jesus, too. Because in the bread and fish they tasted the love that always feeds us, always waters us, always sustains us. A love that weaves joy out of threads of sorrow, and ministry from the bare threads of fatigue. A love that can take the broken shards of fear and grief and doubt, and mend them with grace, and use them for laying a table where all may come, *all* may come, and rest, and eat, and be filled.

Can God set a table in wildernesses of smallness, emptiness, and fatigue? Indeed, it is where she does her best and most abundant culinary magic!

Seventy Times Seven

A Skit

Needed are a Narrator, Peter, Jesus, Peter's Thoughts, Jesus' Thoughts, a King, a Servant, an Other Servant, two Bouncers, four or five Reflectors, and some props: a crown (and perhaps a robe) for the King; posterboard signs for Peter's Thoughts and Jesus' Thoughts that read: "... and I'm thinking...."

At the start, Peter and Jesus are "frozen" and ready for dialogue. Their Thoughts are off to their sides. Whenever the Thoughts speak, they hold up their sign, like a balloon in a cartoon strip. The King and Slave are frozen upstage, right, and the Other Slave is frozen upstage, left. The gallery of Reflectors is seated in front, watching. They will have thought about what they want to say when their turn comes to speak.

Narrator	One day Peter says to Jesus:
Peter	Lord, if my brother or sister sins against me, how often should I forgive? As many as seven times?
Peter's Thoughts	Yeah, right... seven times! The rabbis only allow it *three* times. Anymore than that, and a person looks like he's trying to outdo the mercy of God!
Jesus' Thoughts	He still doesn't get it. They just can't believe this God I know, and the wideness of God's love.

He throws his arms wide open, knocking Jesus off-balance and startling him a bit. He mimes an apology to Jesus.

Peter's Thoughts	Seven times. Ridiculous! There aren't even seven ways to say it: "I forgive you... That's alright... Forget it...." But he'll think I'm cool just for coming up with such a radical idea!

Peter and his Thoughts look proud, "high-five" each other, etc.

Jesus	Actually, Peter, no. Not seven times. More like seventy-seven times!

Peter and his Thoughts are stunned into silence and embarrassed.

Jesus
: You see, Peter, it's like this. In the country of heaven, mercy flows wide and free, like the great old Mississippi River! Imagine a King....

The Narrator begins to talk as Jesus is finishing, so the word "King" is said by each simultaneously. Jesus, Peter, and their Thoughts sit to watch the drama.

Narrator
: There was a King....

: But how he ever got to be king is a mystery, because in matters of money he was clueless. In fact, one of his servants owed him what would amount today to nine million dollars!

The King and the Servant are miming their struggle over the huge amount owed and then the forgiveness of the debt.

Narrator
: Nine million dollars! And there were others who owed him, too. But look what he does with this debt. He writes the whole thing off! Doesn't even suggest a payment plan. Can you imagine a heart so soft? So uncalculating, so unwise, so open? How'd he ever get to be a king?

The Servant is bowing, backwards, away from the King, who is lovingly bidding him farewell. He then addresses the congregation.

Servant
: *Now* what?! Anger I could have dealt with. Wrath! Retribution, like I deserved! But this? Why, he just opened the floodgates of mercy and now...now I'll owe him, some kind of way. I hate that!

Narrator
: Have you ever seen a heart so small and tight? Here is a miracle of grace and he can't let it change him. Not even a little.

Servant
: I have to find some way to pay him back. Then we'll be even. On the scales of life, things have to add up or you can get really hurt!

Narrator
: So off he went to extract the measly pounds of flesh that others owed him!

Servant
: *(seizing the Other Servant by the throat)* You owe me money, you miserable, worthless loser! You'd better pay or I'll have you thrown into jail.

The Other Servant runs all the way around back to the King, and whispers in his ear.

Narrator	Well, when the sad and terrible news of the merciless servant came back to the King, he was furious at first, and demanded the wicked servant to appear before his throne. But when he saw him, his heart just ached...

The King kneels down where the Servant is, takes his hands, and tries to look into his eyes, but the Servant won't do it.

Narrator	because he knew their relationship was broken and there was nothing he could do.

Sadly, the King banishes the Servant from his presence. Peter and the rest return to center stage.

Jesus	*(to Peter)* So will it be for you, Peter, if you do not forgive your brother or your sister, from the heart.
Reflector	*(standing to face the people)* I remember a time when I didn't want to forgive someone. It felt like/it was like.... *(Sits down.)*
Reflector	*(standing to face the people)* I remember a time when someone forgave me and I didn't really deserve it! It felt like/it was like.... *(Sits down.)*
Reflector	*(standing to face the people)* I remember a time when someone refused to forgive me. It felt like/it was like.... *(Sits down.)*
Reflector	*(standing to face the people)* I remember a time I was able to forgive someone. It felt like/it was like.... *(Sits down.)*
Narrator	Imagine what it would have been like in the kingdom that day if the merciless Servant had just opened his heart and let the mercy flow right on through to someone else, who let it flow right on through to someone else, on and on and on. It would have been like a national holiday!
Reflector	It's the only thing you can do with mercy, you know.
Reflector	You can't store it up, or save it, or hoard it.
King	It won't sit still or be contained. It flows, keeping the heart supple and warm.
Peter	My brand of forgiveness is like a score card. Subtract a little trust, add a little distance.

Jesus   But real true forgiveness, from the heart, has forgotten how to count. God's forgiveness is immeasurable, never runs out, never stops, never adds up. It just spills and floods, pours and flows, bringing us home to God's heart.

Servant   I wonder what it would be like to lay down all my fear, and just stand in grace, bathing in the river of mercy that flows from that heart. Maybe I'll try it and see.

FINDING THE LOST

A Tableau Vivant

Needed are a Reader, Jesus, about three to four Scribes and Pharisees, about three to four Sinners, a Shepherd, Little Sheep, about four Other Sheep, who double as the Woman's Friends, and a Woman with a broom.

The beauties of a tableau vivant are that they are easy and quick to prepare, they can use actors of all ages, and the group of actors can come up with its own choreography, although some suggestions follow. In a tableau, worshipers close their eyes and the reading begins. While the reader is reading, the actors are creating a scene. They freeze, a bell is rung, and the worshipers open their eyes and view the scene, in silence, for about ten seconds. The bell is rung again, the worshipers close their eyes again, the reader continues, and the actors get into their next scene, and so on.

The more variety there is in terms of age, gender, posture, height, facial expression, arm positions, and placement of bodies, the more interesting and "real" will be the scene. Even a ladder works well for adding height dimension. Big facial expressions and creative use of hands add interest; you can't overdo it! Quiet music may be played during the tableau.

Ring the bell, have worshipers close their eyes. The reader begins while the actors arrange themselves in the scene.

SCENE ONE

Now all the tax collectors and sinners were coming near to listen to Jesus. And the Pharisees and the scribes were grumbling and saying, "This fellow welcomes sinners and eats with them!"

> *Jesus and the Sinners are gathered around the altar, eating, playing, enjoying each other. The Pharisees and Scribes are stage forward, pointing accusingly, conspiring, grumbling.*

Actors freeze, the bell is rung, and worshipers view the scene. The bell is rung, worshipers close their eyes; the reader and actors proceed as before.

SCENE TWO

So he told them a parable: Which of you, having a hundred sheep and losing one of them, does not leave the ninety-nine in the wilderness and go after the one that is lost until he finds it? When he has found it, he lays it on his shoulders and rejoices. And when he comes home, he calls together his friends and neighbors, saying to them, "Rejoice with me, for I have found my sheep that was lost."

Jesus has left the Sinners up at the altar and come down to talk to the Pharisees and Scribes. He is in front of them pointing down (below the steps) to this scene: A Shepherd has found his lost Sheep (one of the smallest children) and hoisted it on his shoulder, while the other Sheep cling joyfully to his/her legs, waist, etc. They are all headed forward, toward the congregation, inviting them to the feast.

Actors freeze, the bell is rung, and worshipers view the scene. The bell is rung, worshipers close their eyes; the reader and actors proceed as before.

SCENE THREE

Just so, I tell you, there will be more joy in heaven over one sinner who repents than over ninety-nine righteous persons who need no repentance. Or what woman having ten silver coins, if she loses one of them, does not light a lamp, sweep the house, and search carefully until she finds it? When she has found it, she calls together her friends and neighbors, saying, "Rejoice with me, for I have found the coin that I had lost."

Now Jesus is pointing to a new scene: A woman with a broom is holding up a coin in great joy, while her friends rejoice. The Pharisees and Scribes should have placed themselves in new positions.

The bell rings, worshipers close their eyes, and the actors should quickly and quietly disappear. The reader continues:

Just so, I tell you, there is joy in the presence of the angels of God over one sinner who repents.

The bell is rung, and the worshipers open their eyes to a cleared "stage."

Jesus and the Children and the Rich Young Man

Mark places these two events side by side, perhaps so that they light up each other.

You know how it is when you're in the company of children? If you'll let them, they can carry you away to a whole new realm. But you have to get down here, below knee-level, where you can see into their true, clear eyes. Down here, where the impossible is believed, and the truth might be told, in a whisper, in your ear, and a soft touch might heal you.

One day, Jesus was all tangled up with some children, laughing, wrestling, cuddling, drinking up their delicious simplicity, storing up hugs for the lonely, deadly walk that lay ahead of him, when SUDDENLY he is assaulted by a very grown-up adult! Intense, pushy, deadly serious, and hell-bent, it would seem, on "getting it right." Grown-ups, you know, are very intent on "getting it right," which is the *most delicate balance* between trying very hard, and not risking much at all.

And so, rudely snatched from the magic world of the children, Jesus shifts his attention to the serious, tiresome adult world that is pressing in around him, and kneeling there in front of him. "You want to talk theology, scripture, law? Okay, we'll talk. But if you really want to know what's important and true, the answers can be found in these small, holy teachers at our feet!"

Only, the rich and righteous man doesn't even see the children, so captivated and absorbed is he by his own agenda, all the more urgent because it's his, and he is a rich, important grown-up. "See *me*!" he demands. "Engage me in meaningful, adult conversation. But, for God's sake, don't confuse me with anything like the truth!"

While Jesus is quoting Scripture to him ("You know the commandments: You shall not murder, nor steal, nor commit adultery."...) he is sizing him up and seeing right through him, and, with the speed of light, he knows him. And he loves him. He *loves* him. Jesus is struck and surprised with a tender compassion for this young man.

So he doesn't try to reel him in, slowly, with logic and strategy. Caution thrown to the wind, and as ingenuous as the kids still playing at his feet, Jesus offers him the whole thing, the heart of the matter, the truth he needs so he can be free. Jesus offers him the gift of himself.

"Why don't you come with me?" says Jesus. "Your money? Oh . . . well, you could give it away. You aren't going to need it, anyway. Listen! This is an adventure that money can't buy!"

As Jesus watches the rich young man slump and skulk and sputter away, his own heart aches and falls not just a little. And then he sees the children, who are seeing him, and watching and listening hard for the truth that is behind his gaze and under his words.

So, kneeling, he gathers them close, and while their hands are caressing his cheeks, like children do, wondering at the grown-up skin, so different from their own, their touch blesses him. And he blesses them back, giving thanks to the God who has stooped to grant the precious truth of heaven to little ones such as these.

A Reading from Habakkuk

The idea for this kind of congregational reading was borrowed from the Reverend Ernesto Medina. You can write your own!

*The people respond to each sentence or phrase with the words or instructions in **bold print**.*

This is the oracle that the prophet saw. O LORD, how long shall I cry for help?	**HELP!**
and you will not listen? Or cry to you "Violence!" and you will not save?	***(big sigh)***
Why do you make me see wrong-doing, and look at trouble?	***(softly groaning)* Oh, no!**
Destruction and violence are before me!	***(more loudly)* Oh, no!**
Strife and contention arise!	***(loudest yet)* Oh, NO!!**
So the law becomes slack and justice never prevails.	***(sadly)* It never prevails.**
The wicked surround the righteous so that judgment comes forth perverted.	**This is terrible!**
Look at the nations, and see!	**Look and see!**
Be astonished!	***(a gasp)***
Be astounded!	***(a louder gasp!)***
For a work is being done in your days that you would not believe if you were told.	**But tell us, tell us!**
I am rousing the enemy, who march through the earth to seize dwellings not their own.	***(thoughtfully)* Hmmmm.**

There is a long, worried pause.

Are you not from of old, O L ORD my God?

Mighty and eternal?

Why do you look on the treacherous,
and are silent when the wicked swallow
those more righteous than they?

Why, O Lord?

I will keep watch to see what he will say.

Speak, Lord!

The L ORD answered and said, "Write a vision."

(polite clapping)

Make it plain on tablets
so that a runner may read it.

Oh, good!

For there is still a vision for the appointed time.

(louder) **Oh, GOOD!**

It speaks of the end, and does not lie.

(loud cheering and clapping)

If it seems to tarry, wait for it;
it will surely come.

Come soon!

Look at the proud!
Their spirit is not right in them,
but the righteous live by their faith.

**The righteous of God live
by their faith!**

ONE WHO GAVE THANKS: THE STORY OF TEN LEPERS

One storyteller is needed, and ten people to read the parts of the lepers. The lepers can rise from their seats in the nave to read, or could be stationed about the sanctuary in various frozen poses.

Storyteller	Once upon a time there were ten lepers who lived with a bunch of other lepers, in a "No Man's Land" between Samaria and Galilee. The Jews, in those days, hated the Samaritans, and the Samaritans feared the Jews, but not here in this tragic place. Here the lepers lived side by side, Samaritan and Jew, untouchable, unclean, shunned, miserable.
	One day, as Jesus was walking to Jerusalem, he passed by the lepers' godforsaken colony. The Law required that lepers call out to warn others of their nearness, so no one would touch them accidentally, and become unclean himself. So that's what they did. They cried out loudly:
All Ten Lepers	Jesus! Master! Have mercy on us! Have mercy!
Storyteller	They didn't really expect him to stop. It was just something they did when a stranger passed by, a novelty, a diversion. They were ignored every time, but, still, it broke up the numbing, desperate, lonely day.
	Only this time, the stranger did stop. He listened and heard them. He looked at and saw them. He seemed to feel something for them. "Go to Jerusalem," said the strange rabbi, "and show yourselves to the priest." Only a priest, said the Law, could pronounce a leper clean and healed, and lift this terrible curse of the walking dead.
	Now, it can't have been easy to get up and leave that place! To rise in their stiffness and pain, to set forth with all that shame and guilt, to dare to believe. But strange and fearsome though it was to up and leave, somehow they found the courage and imagination, and that's just what they did. And on the way there, they were healed. Which just goes to show you that "on the way" isn't just a no-place

---

LITURGY FOR THE WHOLE CHURCH / SUSAN K. BOCK

between here and there. "On the way" can be an important and healing in-between place all its own, a "someplace."

I wonder if you're there now, somewhere "on the way." If so, take heart. Remember these lepers, and imagine what might be!

As it happened in this story, "on the way" was about a fifty-mile trip, a four- or five-day walk for someone in weak health. The healings, then, would have been slow enough to seem possible, but fast enough to seem like a miracle. Ten lepers were healed "on the way" to Jerusalem.

But one of those lepers had gotten kind of used to being sick. His leprosy was like an old friend, like an old pair of shoes that can't really take you anywhere, but just feel so good you keep them anyway.

First Leper	I never really thought about going back to say "thank you" because now I couldn't be "just a leper." Now I had to be responsible for myself, and maybe others, and I was, like, "Thanks. For nothin'!" When you're used to your affliction, addiction, sorrow, sin, whatever, it's hard to grab hold of life's goodness and joy and say "thanks."
Storyteller	The second leper felt pretty much entitled to the healing she got.
Second Leper	I'd spent a lot of time being angry, complaining, asking, "Why me?" It's hard to say "thank you" when what's on your mind is, "It's about time! It's only what I deserve!"
Storyteller	The third leper was kind of a skeptic—scholarly, bright, a little too sophisticated to believe that there really could be a God who could care enough about us to hear us, heal us, bless us.
Third Leper	It's hard to say "thank you" when you're thinking, "There's got to be a reasonable explanation for all this. Maybe I never really even had leprosy. What's *God* got to do with it?"
Storyteller	The fourth leper, fiercely independent and self-reliant, believed in a God of blessing, but just didn't want to owe God or anyone any thanks, or anything else.
Fourth Leper	"Maybe it's my new diet," I thought, "or positive thinking, or bottled water that made me well." It's hard to say "thank you" when you're always saying, "I can do it myself."

Storyteller	The fifth leper was a very busy person. Or he was, till this illness slowed him down! And he meant to be again if he every got well. So when his skin began to heal, he headed straight for the office and resumed his busy busyness and was soon way overscheduled, like important people are, and forgot all about Jesus.
Fifth Leper	It's hard to go back and say "thank you" when you haven't written it into your Palm Pilot or Franklin Planner. I mean, giving thanks is polite and all, but it's not very useful or profitable. Anyway, I'll get around to it when my schedule clears. Someday.
Storyteller	The sixth leper, when she got well, headed straight for the Home Depot, then Circuit City, then to the mall. And soon she sat in a big, lovely house surrounded by stuff: several fast computers, a flat-screen TV, the latest kitchen appliances, two cars in the garage, a closet full of fine clothes.
Sixth Leper	Sometimes I feel a little uneasy because I don't really own all this stuff. The bank owns it, of course. Owns me, I guess. But I just go buy something else and the discomfort passes. I actually once started back to Jesus to say "thank you," but on the way, there was an outlet mall. With a sale. And I never quite made it.
Storyteller	The seventh leper just didn't think he deserved this healing, was completely unworthy of it.
Seventh Leper	Even God couldn't love me. Even God, if he really knew me, couldn't forgive me, much less shower me with blessings and grace. No one deserves leprosy more than me! It's hard to say "thank you" for the gift when you haven't really accepted it, or you're always trying to give it back.
Storyteller	The eighth leper thought himself reasonable, responsible, and thrifty. He was saving up against an uncertain future.
Eighth Leper	When there was retirement to consider, my kids' educations, that cruise I'd promised my wife, how could I justify the time, the money, the gas, to go back to Jesus just to say "thank you"? It's a lovely idea but, get real! It's completely impractical!
Storyteller	The ninth leper thought that returning to say thanks was a good thing to do but she assumed someone else would take care of it.
Ninth Leper	There were nine others healed, weren't there? One of them will do it. Jesus doesn't need my measly "thank you."

Storyteller	Off they went, each for pretty good reasons of his or her own, too cynical, busy, proud, unworthy, practical, haughty, indebted, whatever, to circle back round to Jesus to say "thank you." Off they went, getting further and further away from the one who'd given them the greatest blessing of their lives.

All but one. He knew his healing was a gift. And if there was a gift, there had to be a giver. And if there was a giver, there was a love that gave. And if there was love, there was the possibility of a relationship. And suddenly he knew that he wanted that relationship more than anything else, even the healing.

So back he went. Right away, first things first. First, give your thanks. Which brought him back to Jesus. Giving his thanks, he got Jesus. He got Jesus, like he never before had dreamed of having anyone. He gave thanks, and he got Jesus!

It might work for you, too. Giving thanks might give you Jesus like never before.

Will he heal and bless you anyway? Absolutely. Just like he did the other nine. Without your thanks, he'll heal and bless you all the same. But finding how to give your thanks might give you him, might give you Jesus, more deeply, more truly, more completely and joyfully, than ever before.

Which leper are you? What's holding you back? How could you let that go, and come back round to Jesus, and get him, have him, like never before? What would it be like to have him, to really have him? |

THE SONS OF ZEBEDEE

A Tableau Vivant

A ladder would be a good addition to this tableau.

The beauties of a tableau vivant are that they are easy and quick to prepare, they can use actors of all ages, and the group of actors can come up with its own choreography, although some suggestions follow. In a tableau, worshipers close their eyes and the reading begins. While the reader is reading, the actors are creating a scene. They freeze, a bell is rung, the worshipers open their eyes and view the scene, in silence, for about ten seconds. The bell is rung again, the worshipers close their eyes again, the reader continues, and the actors get into their next scene, and so on.

The more variety there is in terms of age, gender, posture, height, facial expression, arm positions, and placement of bodies, the more interesting and "real" will be the scene. Even a ladder works well for adding height dimension. Big facial expressions and creative use of hands add interest; you can't overdo it! Quiet music may be played during the tableau.

Ring the bell, have worshipers close their eyes. The reader begins while the actors arrange themselves in the scene.

SCENE ONE

The mother of the sons of Zebedee came to Jesus with her sons, and kneeling before him, she asked a favor of him. And he said to her, "What do you want?" She said to him, "Declare that these two sons of mine will sit, one at your right hand and one at your left in your kingdom."

Jesus and the mother are center-stage, talking privately, with her kneeling and imploring and Jesus looking at the two sons, deep in thought. The sons are up on a ladder, or on two different ladders, looking very exalted and happy. The other disciples are elsewhere, involved with each other in talking, playing, etc. One of them could be eavesdropping on the private conversation.

Actors freeze, the bell is rung, and worshipers view the scene. The bell is rung, worshipers close their eyes; the reader and actors proceed as before.

SCENE TWO

But Jesus answered, "Are you able to drink the cup that I am about to drink?" They said to him, "We are able." He said to them, "You will indeed drink my cup, but to sit at my right hand and at my left, this is not mine to grant, but it is for those for whom it has been prepared by my Father."

> *The brothers will have come down from the ladder(s) and are intensely engaged with Jesus, as in debate. The other disciples will have moved closer, as though listening in, but not really in the center of it. The mother might be up on the ladder (since it is status she was seeking in the first place) and watching, proudly and hopefully.*

> *Actors freeze, the bell is rung, and worshipers view the scene. The bell is rung, worshipers close their eyes; the reader and actors proceed as before.*

SCENE THREE

When the ten heard it, they were angry with the two brothers. But Jesus called them to him and said, "You know that the rulers of the Gentiles lord it over them, and their great ones are tyrants over them."

> *Some of the disciples are gathered around Jesus, who is teaching them from about two or three steps up the ladder. They are sitting, kneeling, standing, listening. The others are engaged in angry "conversation" with the two brothers, accusing, resentful, pushing them down, etc.*

> *Actors freeze, the bell is rung, and worshipers view the scene. The bell is rung, worshipers close their eyes; the reader and actors proceed as before.*

SCENE FOUR

It will not be so among you; but whoever wishes to be great among you must be your servant, and whoever wishes to be first among you must be your slave; just as the Son of Man came not to be served but to serve, and to give his life as a ransom for many.

> *Now Jesus will be seated on the floor, with some of the others on the ladder, while he washes their feet. The rest of the disciples will have reconciled, some just barely, but they are all together in one group.*

> *The bell is rung and worshipers close their eyes. The reader can repeat the above verse, "It will not be so among you . . ." while the actors quickly and quietly disappear. The bell is rung and worshipers open their eyes to a cleared "stage."*

The Tax Collector and the Pharisee

A Dramatic Reading for Two Voices

This story is read by two voices: each one speaks about the other and also for himself. The Tax Collector can be seated at a table with lots of coins stacked up, money bags, a calculator, etc. The Pharisee can be kneeling on the floor with a prayer shawl, a BIG Bible, prayer beads, etc. A ladder is an effective prop, as well, if the Pharisee is able to climb and read at the same time!

The Pharisee is self-righteously pious at first, and the Tax Collector somewhat derisive.

Tax Collector	He knew the Law, that Pharisee. Inside out. And he loved it. He loved it. And he kept it. To the letter.
Pharisee	To me, Moses' Law was sweeter than honey, more precious than gold. So I kept it, alright. Every jot, tittle, and iota.
Tax Collector	Whatever *they* are!
Pharisee	If only everyone else did, then the messiah we'd awaited so long might finally have to come! Well. Anyway. It wasn't going to be *my* misdeed that delayed him. So, I kept my nose to the moral grindstone, and labored away.

Here the Pharisee may frantically search through the scriptures.

Tax Collector	Hey, I knew the Law as well as he did. Once, when I was younger, I'd actually kept it, as perfectly as any Pharisee. I'd longed for the messiah, too, and I used to believe that my righteousness alone could bring him.
Pharisee	I prayed twice a day and fasted twice a week and I was honest and just and cared for the poor. And I tithed.
Tax Collector	He *tithed!* Before taxes!

Pharisee	When I went out into the marketplace, I pulled my cloak tightly around me. And as soon as I got home, I would, of course, do all the ritual washings, in case any uncleanness had brushed up against me.
Tax Collector	Only the Law got harder and harder, and those who could keep it, fewer and fewer, and I sure wasn't one of them.
Pharisee	But even though I filled up my mind with Torah, and filled up my life with good deeds, I just felt so empty, you know? Like a huge clay water pot, waiting to be filled. And I began to think, the messiah's never going to come!
Tax Collector	And if he does it sure won't be to my neighborhood. I decided I just wasn't any good, not by any measure of any law. Sometimes I knew what was right but couldn't do it. Sometimes I could, but just didn't.
Pharisee	For all the loveliness and truth of the Law of Moses, it got so hard to keep.
Tax Collector	For all its breadth and depth, it sure couldn't keep me.
Pharisee	And being that good was awfully lonely! So, every chance I had, I went up to the Temple to pray and I stood there, alone, and lifted up my voice to remind God how well I'd been doing and all the good I'd been up to.
Tax Collector	And then one day I woke up and found myself in a tax office, miles from the Temple and the good folks who prayed there. And I had no idea how to get back.
Pharisee	*(loudly, with arms uplifted)* I thank you, God, that I am not like those others. Or am I?
Tax Collector	So I hadn't been up there in a mighty long time. Moral failings aside, with my work I was always ritually unclean, and there wasn't enough water and blood in all Jerusalem to get me right with God again!
Pharisee	I wondered, Could God even hear me? Did he see how hard I tried and how tired I was? It was like climbing a ladder, you know, one pious thing after another *(climbing a rung with each phrase),* get it right, do good, don't mess up, be perfect.

Tax Collector	*(after a reflective pause)* I'd started hanging around this guy Jesus, a kind of rabbi, only lots more fun. He knew the Law as well as any Pharisee, and he kept it, all the washings and such, but never when it got in the way of loving someone.
Pharisee	*(looking up beyond the ladder's top)* Sometimes I'd think I was getting there, but then at the top there'd be an extension. Again and again. So I'd just grit my teeth and keep on climbing. I didn't know what else to do. But I couldn't help but wonder if there wasn't another way to get right with God.
Tax Collector	Jesus told these great stories that wrapped all around you. And his voice and eyes made a weary soul want to rest and not think so hard about sin.
Pharisee	There's something in the human heart hell-bent on justifying itself, on buying grace, and deserving love—reaching heaven on the ladder of our own merit.
Tax Collector	When I found myself following Jesus up to the Temple to pray, I couldn't believe it! But, well, I couldn't stay away from that man.
Pharisee	And stubborn as we are, some of us climb pretty high. Only we get worn out, *(starting the descent)* and afraid and angry, and then, of course, we fail and fall, and then hide, guilty and ashamed.
Tax Collector	Up at the Temple I stood way back, and kept my eyes down, and my voice small. But I prayed. Yeah, me. *I prayed!*
Pharisee	But what if there is no ladder? Just lots of grace to cover our inevitable failures. And tons of forgiveness. And loads of tender mercy, for everyone, Pharisee and tax-collector, alike?
Tax Collector	*(in a small voice and very humble posture)* Please be merciful to me, God, because I am a sinner, and, heaven help me, I don't know how not to be. But if your mercy is good for anything, it has to be able to save even me. To give me back to myself, and to you, and to everyone else, every morning and every night, again and again and again.
Pharisee	One of the things we do in this sad campaign to justify ourselves is to put everyone into a slot: Pharisee or tax-collector, sinner or saint, good or bad, in or out, right or wrong—as if there wasn't enough of God's love to go around us all.

The Pharisee might here circle the baptismal font, and loudly scoop water to sound with the Tax Collector's next words.

Tax Collector	But you know what I found? There *is* enough. Love enough to *drench the world.*
Pharisee	Maybe there's love enough for the most tainted guilty sinner and the most haughty Pharisee who ever breathed. Maybe, if we could take in just a tiny bit of that enormous love, well, maybe we could let go of the need to save ourselves, to be our own God.
Tax Collector	You know what the rabbis say? That each of us is connected to God by a string. And whenever we mess up, God forgives us. And whenever God forgives us, a knot is tied in the string, bringing us closer, and closer, and closer to God.

Here, they may begin to address each other.

Pharisee	What if there is no ladder?
Tax Collector	Just heartstrings. Divine heartstrings. Holding on tight.
Pharisee	And no real "sinners"...
Tax Collector	and no real saints?
Pharisee	Just the beloved of God...
Tax Collector	being carried home to that heart where we all belong.

For these last two lines, the two will have come close enough, finally, perhaps to reach out to each other.

Pharisee	What if it's true?
Tax Collector	What if we dared to believe it?

Naomi and Ruth

A Dramatic Reading for Two Women

Ruth	"What's in a name?" they say.
Naomi	Only *everything,* I say! Naomi, they called me. *Pleasant.* And so I was, for life was good! An old husband to warm me each night with his love. The strong, handsome sons of my heart. And they'd married well!
Ruth	Not to the "nice Jewish girls" she'd hoped for...
Naomi	but *good* girls, my Ruth and Orpha. Lovely, kind. *Fertile!* Bubby, Nana, Granny—they could call me whatever they liked, so long as they came soon, those grandkids, and filled up my lap and my kitchen!
Ruth	She wasn't your typical mother-in-law, Naomi. More like a sister, wise and respectful. Never bossy or intrusive. But she couldn't resist the little remarks about babies....
Naomi	"Hey, Ruthie, I hear Deborah down the road just got her fifth grandchild!"
Ruth	"How long have you two been married now?"
Naomi	"Oh, nothing. Just a little sweater...you know how I love to knit."
Naomi and Ruth	Life was good...
Naomi	and full and rich...
Ruth	and sweet and sure...
Naomi	and pleasant. But then, when my husband died...
Naomi and Ruth	darkness fell over my heart...
Ruth	when my husband died.

Naomi	No more warmth in the night…
Ruth	or kisses at daybreak.
Naomi	No whispers and dreams,…
Ruth	secrets and plans,…
Naomi	knowing glances.
Ruth	No winks or caresses. No hopes for children…
Naomi	or grandchildren.
Naomi and Ruth	No beloved, or belovedness.

A brief silence follows.

Naomi	Go home, daughter, I said. You still need a husband, and there'll be no more sons from this old womb. Go back to your people, your gods, your mother.
Ruth	But *you* are my mother, I said. Do not make me leave you!
Naomi	But I must go back to my own lands.
Ruth	Then I will go, too!
Naomi	I've no place to stay.
Ruth	Then we'll stay "no place" together.
Naomi	But my people…
Ruth	will be my people.
Naomi	And my God…
Ruth	will be my God.
Naomi	But you will die there, in a land far and foreign…
Ruth	and lie down beside you, in the dust, at my end.
Naomi and Ruth	So together we went…
Naomi	trudging down into Judah, all alone in the world, except for each other,…
Ruth	to Bethlehem, a quaint little town—I wonder if you've heard of it?—

Naomi	arm in arm, my Ruth and I.
Ruth	"You can never go home," they say.
Naomi	Well, you can, I say. But it's not "home" anymore.
Ruth	"Naomi!" they shouted, the women she'd known. "Naomi, you're back, and just look at you! You haven't changed a bit!"
Naomi	What, were they *blind*? I was changed to the bone. Including my name. "Call me Mara," I said. "Bitter. For the Lord has dealt bitterly with me."
Ruth	We just barely scraped by, two women alone. There were days we'd have gladly lay down and die.
Naomi	But life pulls you on, like it or not.
Ruth	So one day, when our bellies growled more than our grief, ...
Naomi	I sent her off to the wheat fields, to glean the grain left from the reaping.
Ruth	And the fields, it turned out, belonged to her cousin Boaz, ...
Naomi	a kind and just man, who opened his heart to our need ...
Ruth	and saved our lives ...
Naomi	and awakened our own hearts to what could be, ...
Ruth	which turned out to be more than we'd dared to hope.
Naomi	When he took Ruth as his wife, the people and elders shouted blessing upon them:
Ruth	"May the Lord make your bride like Rachel and Leah," they said, "giving you children, and a name, in Bethlehem!"
Naomi	And when she laid my grandson in my arms, the women said, rightly, "A daughter who loves you is more than seven sons!"
Ruth	Who can tell what may come of loss and grief, hunger and shame?
Naomi	And what might be born to an old, barren heart?

JESUS AND ZACCHEUS

Zaccheus was the very last person you'd expect a holy man like Jesus to have a thing to do with, much less go home with, and eat with! I mean, there are limits to love, aren't there? Even God's love has standards, boundaries, expectations, and requirements, doesn't it? Don't you have to be baptized, catechized, certified, penitent, have faith, go to church, do good things—*something*—to get God's love?

Zaccheus hadn't done anything to win Jesus' heart. He was a really bad guy, a tax man, hated by his fellow Jews, a traitor, a cheat, a thief, a terrible, horrible, irreligious, godforsaken, unforgivable man! But these are exactly the kind of people whom Jesus seems to love hanging out with, and now, on his way up to the holy city for a holy feast, this so-called holy man has gathered up quite a parade of the unacceptable. Beggars, prodigals, women, lepers, sinners, harlots, foreigners, and worse. And to each and every one he's extended God's own loving-kindness, touching, healing, and blessing each one. Really, it was a scandal!

But Zaccheus loves a scandal, so here he comes to see for himself, this shockingly loving rabbi.

Only he can't get close enough because he's way too short, and the good folks along the parade route are probably squeezing him out, elbowing him in the eye, which doesn't come close to what they'd like to do to him. But Jesus stops right below the tree Zaccheus is perched in. Stops and looks up for him, and finds him.

"Zaccheus, I see you. Come down, hurry down. I want to come to your house!"
>   Yes, you!
>   Yes, today!
>   Yes, right now!

Now you just know that Zaccheus hasn't had dinner guests in forever—he doesn't have any friends! So he never knows that sweet and sacred table fellowship with others where God is host and guest, where you wash, and sit, and give thanks, and bless wine, and break bread, and talk, and eat, together, in peace. No, this is something he never, ever has anymore.

No, Lord. My house isn't ready. (Have you ever said that? My life isn't ready, Lord. I'm not ready. Not me. Not now. No, Lord.)

But Jesus looks up into Zaccheus's eyes and with love draws him down out of hiding.

"I want to go home with you, Zaccheus, to your place, to your life, as ugly and messy and shameful and sad as it may be. I want to stay with you, to eat with you, to be with you."

Well, Zaccheus, who's only ever gotten what he stole or deserved, is so undone by this graceful offer, so completely undone, that he turns his life around, right then and there. You wouldn't believe how he made things right!

The Law required that if you'd cheated someone and were caught, you had to pay back what you'd taken, plus a fifth of the value, as interest. But Zaccheus was giving half of his wealth to the poor, and, with the other half, he was going to give back what he'd stolen, with interest, at the rate of 400 percent! That was crazy! About as crazy as the unmerited love Jesus had held out to him.

Zaccheus was utterly undone and completely remade by that love which was offered to him, not because he asked, or repented, or earned or deserved it, but because that's how God's love is. It looks for us, draws us out of hiding, sets us free from sin, and gives us back to ourselves and others. And it's for absolutely everyone. Which is scandalous! It *is*. It's a scandal! It scandalized the Pharisees back then and it scandalizes us now down in our small hearts, where we like to keep track of things and believe it should all add up and come out even (but God help us if it ever did!).

But that's what grace is. It's scandalously graceful! It makes no sense, and it's wholly undeserved and it's for absolutely everyone.

And when we finally get it, finally accept it, it's like living in a whole other universe, a universe of abundance, where forgiveness and mercy and love flow abundantly for us and through us and we give ourselves away, not in measured percentages but in unmeasured, scandalous abundance.

Imagine yourself as Zaccheus today. It shouldn't be too hard. Each of us has a hiding place from where we look on, feeling outside, wanting in, thinking we're unworthy, or invisible, or not needed, or it's too late. But Jesus is looking for us, seeking out each one of us for the intimacy he longs to enjoy with us. He will find us, call out our name, gather us close, sit with us and eat in a feast of healing love, just like he did Zaccheus, even Zaccheus, even such a one as him, a really bad guy, whom Jesus loved anyway, just as he was.

This love, this abundant, generous, graceful, lavish love is offered to you, even you, just as you are. Imagine the abundant, generous, graceful, lavish response you could make, and then dare to find the abundant joy of doing it!

THE TEN BRIDESMAIDS

In a village in Palestine, a wedding is a huge celebration, to which everyone is invited, all are welcomed, and most are expected to come. It can last for days, even up to a week! It is a long, lush, liquid relief from the dry tedium of daily life, something about which you'd never say to your spouse, after checking your watch late one Saturday afternoon, "Oh no, honey! We have that wedding tonight!"

In a village in Palestine, as the wedding approaches, the bridesmaids go to the bride to keep her company while she awaits her groom. No one knows when he'll come. It could be tomorrow or two weeks from now, or maybe even tonight! No one knows. Only the groom, and he's not telling, because it is a great trick, in a village in Palestine, to catch the women asleep!

So, if he could, he'd sneak up with stealth, in the quiet cover of night! But custom demands he send a herald who goes ahead through the streets shouting, "Look! Here is the bridegroom! Come out to meet him!" And all the village does, and the bridesmaids, too (if they're awake!), and they all dance and sing the groom to his bride. Then the doors are shut, and the wedding begins, and latecomers just miss out.

Jesus told this parable. The kingdom of heaven is like a great wedding banquet with ten of the bride's closest girlfriends in attendance, wearing gowns she promised could be worn again! And as they waited, they gossiped and giggled and gorged themselves on little puff pastries and quiches and other "girl foods." But as minutes stretched into hours, and hours into days, they got restless and sleepy and testy, and they drifted off into "little naps," they said. Surely they'd hear, with all that commotion (you know how men are, so rowdy and rude!) and curling all up in a soft warm heap, they'd slept.

When the noise was first heard it was part of their dreams, but then they sat bolt upright and scrambled for shoes and sweaters and lamps, and extra oil, just in case they ran out, for the flames were quite low, now, no more than a flicker. "Wait! I need more," said one, and, "Me, too," "So do I," "I've run out!"

"But we've only enough for ourselves" said a few, "and we'll just barely make it with that. No, we can't give you ours. But run to that merchant down the street—there's a sale, I think—and we'll meet you on the road! Hurry!"

So they did. But while they were gone, everyone else came in, and the wedding began. And the joy was so loud that when the unprepared bridesmaids returned no one heard them knocking and pleading, "Let us in, please! Don't start without us!"

The kingdom of heaven, said Jesus, will always surprise you, so be ready: Have oil for your lamps, and keep awake!

Sheep and Goats and the Very Last Day

A Skit

Needed are a narrator, Jesus, a small group of angels, lots of sheep, and lots of goats. Also, a throne, and some costuming, like sheeps' ears and wool, goats' beards and horns, etc.

Narrator   When the Son of Man comes in his glory, and all the angels with him...

Jesus enters with a leap and great flourish. He looks around and realizes he is alone.

Narrator   **and all his angels with him!**...

Jesus   Hey, y'all! Come on!

Unkempt angels enter, with ipods, cell phones, sunglasses, etc., partying, laughing, raucous. Jesus looks worried while heading to his throne.

Narrator   then he will sit on the throne of his glory.

He sits, with pride and excitement.

Narrator   And all the people of all the nations will be gathered before him.

While Jesus looks stage right and left, with happy anticipation, the sheep and goats stray in, making lots of racket, butting each other, etc. The angels quickly retreat to behind the throne, where they will stay, safely out of the way to watch the whole drama. Jesus looks increasingly distraught.

Narrator   And he will separate them from each other, as a shepherd separates the sheep from the goats.

Jesus separates them with great difficulty, using his body, his staff, whatever, while angels look on, giving unhelpful advice and encouragement. Finally, the sheep are to the right of the throne and the goats are to the left, with the occasional stray animal, each flock contentedly grazing, napping, watching what will happen.

Narrator   And he will say to the sheep:

Jesus   Come, sheep! From the very beginning of the world, a special place has been made ready for you...

Sheep rouse and gather round, panting, baaing, butting their heads on Jesus' legs. The goats continue to munch and butt, unaware, mean to each other, etc.

Jesus   with the greenest grass, and the coolest clear water!

Sheep continue to express excitement.

Jesus   For I was hungry and you gave me food! I was thirsty, and you gave me something to drink!

The sheep begin to look at each other questioningly, and to back away, miming, "Did you? Me neither. No, not me."

Jesus   I was a stranger and you welcomed me. I was naked and you clothed me.

Jesus   Sheep continue to back away and hide.

Jesus   When I was sick you cared for me, and when I was in prison, you came to see me!

Jesus looks very pleased and happy, but then notices the sheep are all gone.

Narrator   And the sheep will say:

Sheep   Baaaa, baaaa, baaaa *(and so on)*.

Narrator   Which means:

Sheep   *(as the sheep nervously approach Jesus)* Lord, when did we see you hungry and give you something to eat, or thirsty and give you something to drink? And when did we see you naked and clothe you? When did we visit you in prison?

Narrator   And the Son of Man will say:

Jesus   Listen up!

Sheep gather around and pick up their ears, leaning close to hear.

Jesus	Whenever you did these things—these kind, good, and just things—to any member of my family, you did them to me. And especially when you did them to the hungriest, smallest, and saddest of all the members of my family, you did them to me.
Narrator	Then he will say to the goats, Depart from me, you bad goats!

Sheep rise up and point to goats, chanting: "Baaaadd, baaaddd, baaadd!"

Jesus	For I was hungry, and you gave me no food. I was thirsty, and you gave me nothing to drink. I was a stranger, and you did not welcome me, naked and you did not clothe me, sick and in prison and you did not visit me.
Narrator	And the goats will say:
Goats	Naaaa, naaaa, naaaa *(and so on).*
Narrator	Which means:
Goats	Lord, we were always so busy! We were up at the church just about every night! And, besides, how were we supposed to know it was *you*? All those people, so hungry, sad, and scared. They didn't look like you or act like you. They didn't even come to church!
Narrator	And the Son of Man will say:
Jesus	If you'd taken the time to see them, to look into their eyes, you'd have seen all kind of things. You'd have seen yourselves, and all your own need. If you'd truly looked into their faces, and listened deeply to their sadness, then you'd have felt your hearts expand with my love, and you'd have known I was there with you, in them.

Sheep come over to the goats and minister to them in the way Jesus is describing.

Jesus	In every kindness, every mercy, every act of justice, no matter how small, I myself am there, loving my people, sheep and goats alike.

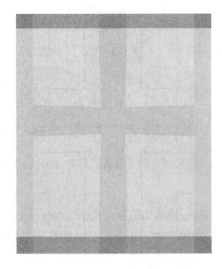

ALL SAINTS

God, whose love
has begotten us:

Trouble the waters
deep in our souls
and help us remember
our baptism.

Stir up the fiery embers
by which
you have marked us
as your own,
and enflame us
with love for the world.
Amen.

A Reading from Ecclesiasticus
with the Remembrance of the Dead

The reading should be distributed throughout the congregation with different persons assigned to stand, when it's time, and loudly read the name of one saint. Add to or change the saints in each category as you choose.

Reader	Let us now sing the praises of the famous, our ancestors in their generations. God apportioned to them great glory, and majesty from the beginning.
	Some were rulers, and made a name for themselves by their valor:
Various Voices	Diana of Wales Elizabeth of Hungary Abraham Lincoln Emma and Kamehameha
Reader	Some led the people by good council, by their knowledge of the people's lore, by their wise words of instruction:
Various Voices	Mother Teresa Dag Hammarskjöld Oscar Romero Evelyn Underhill
Reader	Some spoke in prophetic oracles:
Various Voices	Martin Luther King, Jr. Sojourner Truth Mahatma Ghandi John Lennon

Reader	Some composed musical tunes or put verses in writing:
Various Voices	Julian of Norwich James Weldon Johnson George Herbert e.e. cummings
Reader	All these were honored in their generation, and were the glory of their times. There are some of them who have left a name, so that we all declare their praise. And there are some who have left no memorial, who have perished as though they had not lived.

A brief silence is observed. The people may be invited to remember their own beloved departed, silently or aloud.

Reader	And there were people of mercy, whose righteous deeds have not been forgotten. Their prosperity will remain with us, and with their descendants, and the inheritance of their good lives will trickle down to their children's children. Their followers stand by the covenant with God, as do their children, also, for their sake.

Here, another reader may read the names of all who have died in the past year.

Reader	Their posterity will continue forever, and their glory will not be blotted out. Their bodies were buried in peace and their names live to all generations. Peoples will declare their wisdom, and the congregation will proclaim their praise.

A Sermon for All Saints Sunday

All saints? How can it be?
      Can it be me,
      holy and good,
      walking with God?
How can we say that we're all saints?
      O that we could!

All saints! —Crucified love
      Sings from above
      What it will do
      Making us new,
Naming and claiming us "all saints,"
      till it comes true.

Some Saints touch the divine,
      and as they shine,
      candles at night,
      holy and bright
Gladden the spirits of all saints,
      giving us light.

All saints stumble and fall.
      God, loving all,
      knowing our shame,
      longs to reclaim:
Standing or falling we're all saints.
      Treasure the name!

Come, saints, crowds who have gone
      beckon us on,
      hindrances shed,
      joy in our tread,
one in the Spirit with all saints,
      looking ahead. *

Look around you. This room is crowded with saints.

There are old saints, tiny saints, crabby saints, saintly saints. Black, brown, pink, and peach saints. There are saints who stumble and fall, struggling with shame and regret and confusion, and the saints who are always confident and happy. There are saints brave enough for anything, and saints who are afraid to crawl out of the bed each day. There are saints who feel lost and saints who lead us home. There are saints who can sing and saints who are tone deaf; saints who forgive and saints who hold grudges. Right here, in this room, there are saints who fight each day the temptation to drink, or to give in to despair, and saints for whom life just seems to flow with ease.

This room is crowded with saints! Take a moment to look around you and feast your eyes on this huge crowd of the saints of God, each and every one made glorious and beautiful by the love God has for each of them.

Now, close your eyes, and listen with your heart, and see if you can hear that "crucified love," singing down on you from above, making us new, naming and claiming us all saints until we believe that it's true!

And, with your eyes still closed, look around for all the saints of that crowd who have gone before us: husbands, wives, mothers, grandmas, grandpas, dear friends, and even some of our children. Can you see them hovering just above our heads, all their sorrows shed, their faces lit with laughter? And can you hear them, beckon us on? Listen with your heart. . . .

"Children of God!" they're saying. "Claim that love which is yours! Let it bring you joy. Let it make you brave. Dare to believe that, standing or falling, you *are* all saints. Treasure the name. Saint. Saint. Treasure it."

And now, in your mind's eye, look up just a bit higher and see all those Saints with a capital "S": Saints Matthew and Paul and Peter and Teresa and Constance and Absalom and Martin. They're all here, too! Can you see them? All those saints who touch the divine, making them shine like candle flames, lighting our path, and lifting our hearts in hope.

This room is jam-packed full with saints. Every tiny corner is filled with the glory of the children of God! It's always that way, we just don't notice. But today we stop to take notice of the communion of saints, filling our hearts and our lives.

The famous contemplative monk Thomas Merton had a great definition of the church: "Here comes everybody," he said.

Here comes everybody!

I'm not sure exactly what he meant by that. I'm sure, at the least, he meant that the church makes room for everybody. Gays and straights and old and young and black and white and rich and poor. But maybe, too, he meant to say that only with everybody will God's heart finally be full and God's joy be complete.

If there are baptisms, add:

[Today we are adding several new somebodies to that blest communion which will one day be everybody. *(They should be named.)* The newest saints of God! Each one today is rescued from the kingdom of death, and grafted forever into the kingdom of life from which nothing can ever steal them away. Each one today is ordained to the ministry of Jesus, which is this: to go out looking for *anybody* who needs to be gathered into the *everybody* that we are becoming through the grace of God's love.]

Brothers and sisters, each of you is part of that "everybody," the church. Each of you is called to do the one thing in this world, and for this world, that only you can do. Each one of you is gifted for that work. You were ordained in your baptism. You became priests in your baptism. You are the priests. Those who are ordained priests in the church are only a reminder of your priesthood. You are the priests. You are the saints.

What makes us all saints is not that we are good or right or brave or strong. What makes us saints, quite simply, is that God wants it so, because of God's love and desire for us. What makes us saints is sharing the life of faith, and faith is nothing more or less than saying "Yes" to that love. Saints and children of God, say "Yes" to it. Come home to it. And go into the world dressed and adorned in it, filled and afire with it, so you may bring others home to it, too. Amen.

The Prayers of the People for All Saints Day,
Saints' Days, or Baptismal Feasts

When this form is used, certain petitions may be omitted and others written, as appropriate, for the particular people gathered.

With the help of the Saints of God, let us pray.

That we, like Andrew, would have the love to come and go when you call, we pray to you, Jesus;
Help us to follow.

That we, like Matthew, would find a right relationship to all that we own, we pray to you, Jesus;
Help us to follow.

That we, like Mary, would let you be born in us, and stay close to you all of our lives, we pray to you, Jesus;
Help us to follow.

That we, like Luke, would bring healing in your name to all who are sick or hurt, and that these, especially, would know your loving help: *[names are added here,]* we pray to you, Jesus;
Help us to follow.

That we, like Peter, would keep growing in faith, and together become the church who bravely confesses you, we pray to you, Jesus;
Help us to follow.

That those who are to be baptized or confirmed, being built like living stones into your church, would find your help to grow: *[names are added here,]* we pray to you, Jesus;
Help us to follow.

That we, like John, would walk in the light, and see the City of God in our hearts, we pray to you, Jesus;
Help us to follow.

That we, like Mary Magdalene, would boldly proclaim your resurrection to the frightened and heart-sick, we pray to you, Jesus;
Help us to follow.

That we, like Thomas, would recognize doubt as the seed of true faith, and lead the doubting to touch your love, we pray to you, Jesus;
Help us to follow.

That we, like Paul, might tell the world about you, and, at our end, bravely face death as the doorway to life, we pray to you, Jesus;
Help us to follow.

That these, especially, who have died, would grow forever in grace: *[names are added here,]* we pray to you, Jesus;
Help us to follow.

That we, like Lydia, would open our hearts and homes in welcome, we pray to you, Jesus;
Help us to follow.

That we, like Francis, would tenderly care for your precious creation, we pray to you, Jesus;
Help us to follow.

That we, like Clare, would follow our hearts, no matter what, we pray to you, Jesus;
Help us to follow.

That we, like Harriet Tubman, would lead your people to freedom, we pray to you, Jesus;
Help us to follow.

That we, like Bishop Schereschewsky, would travel far, or sit still with our work, as the Spirit leads, we pray to you, Jesus;
Help us to follow.

The people may add prayers for saints of their choosing, as such prayers rise in their hearts, or they may simply name the saints who have guided them toward God.

That we, like N., would..., we pray to you, Jesus;
Help us to follow.

The prayers conclude with this collect.

Holy One, there are so many whose heroic love remains unsung. Philip and James, Joanna and Susanna, Barnabas and Matthias. That we, too, might live as disciples, brave and true, day by day, we pray to you, Jesus.
Help us to follow. Amen.

SCRIPTURAL INDEX